TA SMALL
TALL SHIP

I

II

TALES FROM A SMALL TALL SHIP

FORTY YEARS OF PLAYING BOATS

BILL McNAUGHTON

III

Acme Pack Diistributing and Publishing Co
38035 Buck Rd. N.E.
Hansville, Wa. 98340

Library of Congress Cataloge Card Number
95-83518

ISBN 0-9650320-0-0

Printed by Mc Naughton & Gunn, Inc.

Cover *Following Seas* by Rob McNaughton

Illustrations by the author

CONTENTS

MAPS
and
ILLUSTRATIONS

MAPS

ILLUSTRAIONS

PHOTOGRAPHS

Cover art
Following Seas
By
Robert McNaughton

TO
"CAPTAIN DINGHY"
KATHY, KENNY, VICKY, CHRIS, SHANNA
AND MY KIDS

AND ALL THE GREAT TEAM
THAT HAS WORKED
OVER THE YEARS
AT
DAD'S MARINE

VIII

ACKNOWLEDGMENTS

I want to thank my son Rob whose computer expertise and computer art got me started on this project, Jack and Lou Mallinckrot who got this book out of irons and headed downwind to the finish line and Kitty James, editor of Santana Magazine, whose final editing made it look like I could write in English.

X

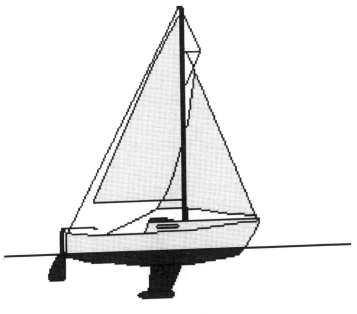

CAL 20

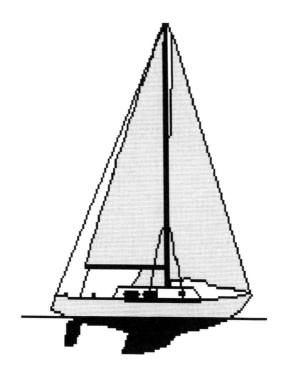

ERICSON 32

ODIN

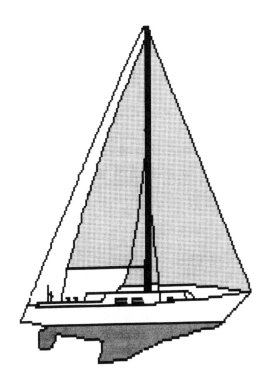

NEWPORT 41
SWIFT

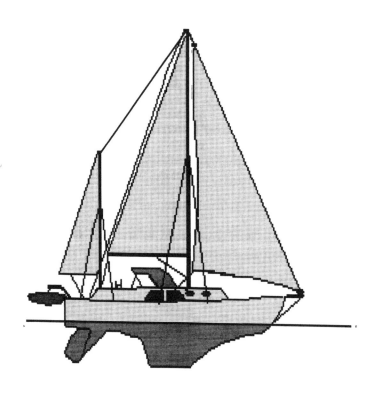

IRWIN 42

SUNLIT

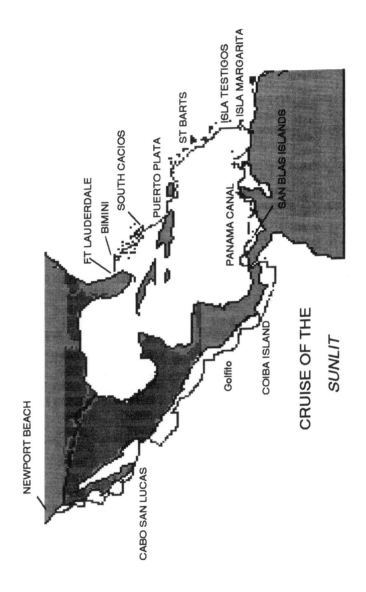

NEWPORT BEACH

CABO SAN LUCAS

FT LAUDERDALE
BIMINI
SOUTH CACIOS
PUERTO PLATA
ST BARTS
ISLA TESTIGOS
ISLA MARGARITA

Golfito
COIBA ISLAND
PANAMA CANAL
SAN BLAS ISLANDS

CRUISE OF THE
SUNLIT

IWALANI

A SMALL TALL SHIP

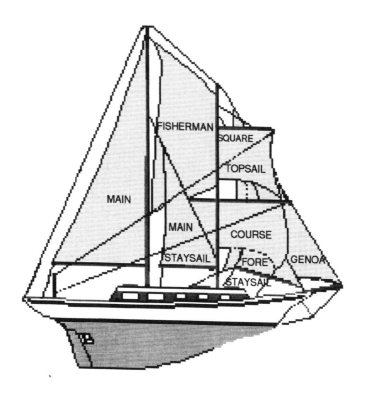

CHEOY LEE

CLIPPER 42

PROLOGUE

"It's an unorganized mess," Jack said to me as he went over the early drafts of my book *TALES FROM A SMALL TALL SHIP*. "You haven't tied it together at all. The punctuation is all wrong and even your poem, *FOLLOWING SEAS*, doesn't have a tie into the book. It's all kind of a hodge podge."

"I know, I know," I replied." But I am going to fix that. I'll find somebody who can punctuate a sentence. I'm not trying to write a chronological biography, there have been many cruising stories told. That would be boring. I want to tell the stories of the exciting things that I have run across on the water and in my store, Dad's Marine. These things just don't fit into a straight time line. Frankly, I don't know what order they all happened. They are special little tales and I think they could fill a book. As for the poem, I like it and I'll put it where I damn well please. I'm looking for constructive encouragement, not criticism."

"Thanks for the help." I continued, "I know I need a lot of it, but in the meantime, I'm going to spend a week in Catalina on *Iwalani* and see if I can sort it out. I'll see you in seven days."

And that is what got me out of my store for a single handed trip to Catalina.

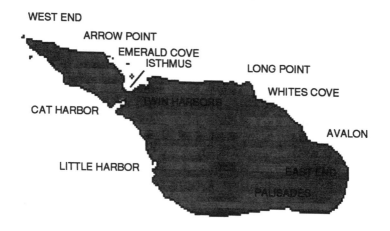

WEST END

ARROW POINT

EMERALD COVE
 ISTHMUS

LONG POINT

WHITES COVE

CAT HARBOR

AVALON

LITTLE HARBOR

SANTA CATALINA ISLAND

1
WHITES COVE

The crossing from Newport to Whites Cove on Catalina had been a normal but still an uncomfortable five an a half hour bash to windward under power and sail. Winds started light but were close to 25 knots just before we eased under the lee of Long Point. *Iwalani*, my small tall ship did her usual good job of breasting the short steep seas that had built up over the long rollers coming in from the West. Her foredeck was washed clean, but little spray had reached the cockpit and I was warm and dry.

Being under power, I had set only her three lower sails: main, main staysail and fore staysail. All have self tending booms and single sheets which make the boat easy to single hand. Even though *Iwalani* is rigged as a brigantine schooner, with yards and square sails on the foremast, her small sized sails and wide decks make her a good boat for short-handed sailing.

I don't single hand very much but this trip was special. I felt it was time for a few days rest away from Dad's Marine, my marine hardware store that has been the source of many of the tales I am about to relate. This book is a kind of summation of 40 years playing boats, and 10 years of selling hardware and giving advice to all the varied and interesting people who have crossed my path over the years. The purpose of this trip was to get my thoughts together and develop an organized story for this book.

My first concern, after picking up a mooring off Button Shell Beach under Long Point, was checking out the inside of the boat. I hadn't been below for about three hours due to the need for steering in the rough chop. There had been a small crash or two down below during that period.

I found the trawler lamp on the floor with only a slight smell of kerosene on the rug. Amazingly the glass chimney was unbroken and the brass shade only slightly dented. A nut had come loose from the bolt on which it was hung. The small rug on the floor was soaking wet which explained the lack of a strong kerosene smell. An immediate check of the bilge found the water even with the floorboard and in the rough seas it had sloshed over onto the cabin sole.

I pumped the bilge and did a thorough check for leaks but could not find any problems. I sat back with a beer in hand and tried to understand what had happened. I soon realized the culprit must have been an open valve on the head which allowed water to overflow when we heeled over in the rough seas, but as soon as we were safely moored, the water subsided back to a normal level and showed no sign of its attempt to sink us.

Note for next time, keep the valves closed and check the bilge more often. Not bad words to live by. "Keep your valves closed and check the bilge."

* * * * * * * * * *

It's hard not to learn something every time you go sailing. So far I have learned to keep the valves closed, but I remember an instance where it was a closed valve that caused all kinds of havoc and earned a man the name of "Captain Dinghy."

CAPTAIN DINGHY

Carter is a trusted friend of mine, and I had just sold him a brand new eight foot dinghy and a three and a half horsepower motor. We met on my dock for an initial trial run. Now Carter was a very knowledgeable sailor and had owned many outboards in the past. I secretly believe he wanted to show me that the product I sold him wasn't as good as I had touted and this evil intent in him was the cause of the events that happened next.

As I held the boat alongside the dock Carter hopped in to show me how hard it was to start. He pulled several times on the starting rope with no results. I, of course, was worried about a good sale of a boat and motor gone bad.

As he spat out a cuss word or two I reached over and innocently asked if the gas valve was turned on and at the same time turned the valve. On his next pull Captain Dinghy became famous. When the engine wouldn't start, he had turned the throttle up with each pull and it was now at full thrust with no neutral.

Well, the engine started. Captain Dinghy, who by this time was standing up in the boat, pitched over the stern and grabbed the gunwale, hanging on for dear life. My grip on the boat had been light and I almost went in the drink as the boat tore away.

My hold and Capt's fall did manage to tip the boat enough to fill it with water, but the engine still roared as it headed down the channel with Captain Dinghy being dragged like a wounded whale along side.

It was almost 50 yards down the channel before he was able to reach up and kill the throttle. That took more strength than I ever had. It was a sad looking man who dragged the boat back to the dock.

We were all relieved that he was not cut by the motor nor had he drowned. I think it took him almost 20 minutes before he could join in the laughter at the incident. I guess the lesson here is not to cuss before you check your valves.

"Captain Dinghy" is still a very good friend of mine. At present he is cruising the Caribbean Sea in his lovely double-ended cutter. I hope he will still be a friend after he reads this book.

* * * * * * * * * *

As I sat back my mind turned to the present. It was the first week of May and, because it was only Thursday, there were only two other boats in the anchorage. After pumping out the boat, tying down the sails and cracking another beer, I relaxed in the cockpit gazing on the green hillsides.

The sun dropped early behind the steep cliffs of Catalina and in just a few minutes I spotted three goats working their way down the path to the beach. This was Catalina at it's best.

The island is famous for the animals that roam its rugged hillsides. Buffalo are often seen in the meadows and goats seem to like the cliffs above Whites and Goat Harbor, just to the west around Long Point. However, the ferocious wild pig is the one true game animal on the island. As I sat in the cockpit of *Iwalani*, I remembered the only encounter I have had with such a terrible animal.

*　*　*　*　*　*　*　*　*　*

I had been hiking up the draw behind the Girl Scout camp when a great rustling of the bushes made me stop in my tracks. I stood petrified as one of those ferocious beasts lumbered towards me. I was afraid to turn my back and run and could only stand ready to make a leap to one side as he came by. I was scared. Snorting and grunting the wild boar came at me and just as I was ready to jump to avoid the attack, the great beast turned sideways rolled over on it's back and begged to have its belly scratched. This infamous wild boar happened to be the camp pet. It would be difficult for me to go wild game hunting on this island.

*　*　*　*　*　*　*　*　*　*

The memory of that encounter gave me a good laugh as I finished my beer and went below to warm a can of spaghetti for supper. That, along with some bread and coffee, would make my meal. I am not a gourmet cook but the length of my belt indicates I eat well. I was looking forward to a beautiful evening and a quiet night.

As I watched the stars grow brighter, even with the soft glow of Los Angeles in the background, I told myself that this really was a great way to relax and get away from the rigors of work at Dad's Marine. The trip over had been tiring but now I had the windward work behind me and could look forward to peaceful days and short sails for the next five or six days until it would be time to head back to what some people call the real world. Personally, I think this is the real world and all the fake stuff lies back on the mainland.

It was easy to lay back and try to piece together the ideas that had eluded me back on the mainland. Stories flooded my mind that I'm sure could be added to my little book that I have bandied about for such a long time. It seemed so simple. I'll just start at the beginning.

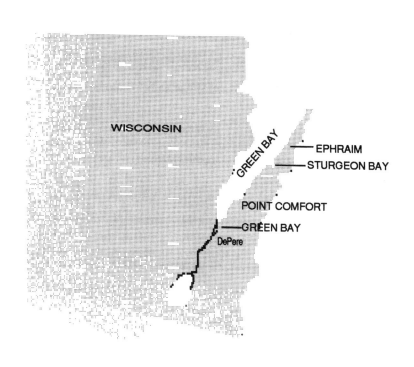

WISCONSIN

GREEN BAY

EPHRAIM
STURGEON BAY

POINT COMFORT

GREEN BAY

DePere

10

HOW IT ALL BEGAN

I have been sailing for well over forty years and I still remember my first cruise, ever, under sail. I was 15 years old and had spent the summer racing as crew on an 18 foot. Seagull sloop under the burgee of the Green Bay, Wisconsin Yacht Club. The skipper, who was about 16, asked me to join him on a trip from Green Bay to Ephraim, A lovely little resort town above Sturgeon Bay. This would be a long trip in an open cockpit, centerboard sloop.

We planned to stop along the way and camp on the beach each night. The first night we pulled into Emil Fisher's little stone wharf. We tied the boat there and spent the night sleeping on the porch of the Branson cottage at Point Comfort. The next day gave us a fine sail up past the entrance to Sturgeon Bay where we pulled into a very small breakwater to have a bit of lunch. If the weather stayed good it would be an hour or so to Ephraim.

But the weather would not cooperate. As we finished our sandwiches the wind went to the north west and built up a heavy chop. The owner of the breakwater told us we would have to leave as he needed to move his own boat into the mooring, which only held one boat. We had to leave and, as it was too wild to go to weather, we reached off toward Sturgeon Bay.

This was exciting sailing and we surfed along at a good clip with five and six-foot seas building up behind us. The entrance to Sturgeon Bay is a wide funnel shaped bay with high cliffs on each side. This funnel has a great effect on the wind and waves. Surfing in the 18 foot Seagull sloop was fun as each wave carried us along for a while and then moved ahead as we slid down the back side. We seemed to be doing well for two or three miles, but then the funnel effect caught us.

I had read about plowing a ship under in the novel, *Captains Courageous,* how an overpowered boat could literally be sailed under by her own speed. Here we were, watching each wave pass under our hull, having a great sail. Then a gust of wind hit us just as we planed along the top of the wave. This time the bow of the boat pointed down the face of the wave and picked up speed.

The wave was over seven feet high and we must have been doing over 15 knots as we tore down the face. The wave ahead of us was a straight wall, and this time instead of lifting up we sailed right through it. We were a submarine. The skipper yelled at me to let go the main halyard. We were awash in the water and before I could undo the tightly jammed cleat he climbed over and cut the halyard through with his sheath knife. Down came the sail all over me as we wallowed in the sea completely swamped.

Fortunately the boat had positive flotation and would not sink. It took about five minutes to get the sail tied down and start to bail. A 22 square meter sloop, under jib only, hove to under our lee and yelled to make sure we were OK. They had seen our shipwreck and were there to help. Another large power boat stopped nearby to help if needed. This was very reassuring to us, but by this time we were under control and able to wave them off. We could make it on our own.

It is said that the best bilge pump in the world is a scared man with a bucket. And we proved it. The boat was soon cleared of water and floating high. Now we still had to get into the harbor, and without a main halyard all we could set was the jib. This was fine for a while as the wind was still blowing hard, but within about thirty minutes we were in the lee of the land and the wind died. We made slow progress for the next hour and it was near dark before we pulled into the Sturgeon Bay Yacht Club dock.

We were a bedraggled couple of kids. Fortunately, our near disaster had been described earlier by the crew of the 22 square meter to the club manager, and he gave us the keys to the club house where we were allowed to sleep on the couches.

We were just turning in when I saw a small runabout drift up to the dock only a few feet from the window, and as I watched the skipper tried the engine starter. A ball of flame shot across the dock as the boat exploded. We raced outside and I grabbed a small child from the arms of the skipper and pulled him out of the boat. Fortunately there was a hose next to us on the dock and that made short work of the fire. The skipper had only minor burns and his son was unhurt.

13

The boat was a mess but we saved it from serious damage. Apparently the engine had stopped out in the basin and gas had leaked into the bilge. After paddling to the dock the owner tried to start it again and the resulting *woomph* of exploding gas was a sound hard to forget.

The next day was Saturday, and we were asked to join the sailboat race that afternoon. We of course agreed and with a fleet of Lightnings, Snipes and another Seagull, we had fine sailing until the wind died, leaving us drifting out in the bay. To bring us in, the commodore of the yacht club motored out in his beautiful 65 foot schooner. The sight of that ship, with men in the rigging, silhouetted against the evening sky, could quite probably be the start of my love of schooners and tall ships.

That night at the trophy party we were introduced to the whole group as the shipwrecked heroes of the boat fire and were honorary guests. Heady stuff for a fifteen year old.

The rest of the cruise was uneventful and we never did reach Ephraim. Instead we headed back toward Green Bay on Monday, spending the night pulled up on the beach. We slept under the sail on the sand. The next afternoon we were drifting under the hot sun, a few miles out from Green Bay, when the skipper's dad arrived in a borrowed outboard to tow us back to the club and home. I remember my first cruise as a very successful one.

* * * * * * * * * *

Since my first cruise at the age of 15, sailing has been a passion. For many years I have raced sail boats. Crewing on boats like Jack's Rhodes 33, Olson 35 yawls and later *Swift,* Jack's Newport 41, a top ocean racing sloop. I also owned about six different sailboats from my first 27 foot wooden cutter, a Cal 20, Ericson 26 and then *Odin*, an Ericson 32.

The ketch *Sunlit* carried us on a two-year trip through the Panama Canal to Florida. A few years later I purchased *Iwalani,* my small tall ship. I raced these boats in club races around Newport and Long Beach and every now and then won something. I have a few trophies in my den.

I also did my share of cruising to Catalina and the Channel Islands of Southern California This sailing was culminated by the two-year cruise in the Irwin 42, *Sunlit*, with my wife and three kids, Laura, Heather and Rob. We sailed from Newport Beach, California, through the Panama Canal to Florida. We often spent three weeks to a month in various ports along the way. We sailed the long beat from Panama through the San Blas Islands to Cartagena, Columbia, the Dutch Leeward islands, Venezuela to Grenada.

From Grenada it was a reach and a run through the West Indies, Puerto Rico, and the Bahamas to Fort Lauderdale, Florida. This trip is a source of many of the tales for this book.

My experience on the ocean has given me a lot of confidence but also a great deal of respect for the sea. It is this respect that has made me look in wonderment at some people I have met that plan to cruise in small boats.

* * * * * * * * * *

Back in the present, darkness was taking over the cove. I could just barely make out the shoreline. It was time to hit the sack. Tomorrow I planned to head up to the Isthmus, or Twin Harbors as they call it now. If the wind was right, I would sail but, I don't mind cranking up the Perkins diesel when the wind doesn't cooperate. One last turn around the deck to check the mooring lines and make sure the boat was secure then I dropped down into the cabin to get ready for a hopefully calm night.

BOAT BANGERS

It is not always calm in Whites Cove. I have had a few bad experiences while moored here. The first time I ever went to Catalina was almost a disaster. I was sailing an old wooden boat, the cutter *Southwind*. This was the first boat I owned in California.

With two friends as crew we left San Pedro for a daysail on a Saturday morning and reached offshore for about an hour. It was a beautiful day. Catalina stood out sharply on the horizon. One of my crew suggested we sail over to Catalina for the weekend. I had no idea what was involved so I readily agreed.

The four-hour trip was a lot longer then planned and we were all very tired when we arrived. After dropping our anchor in about sixty feet of water just to the left of the Girl Scout Camp, we ate the few sandwiches we had and went to sleep curled up in the sails because we didn't have any sleeping bags aboard. The wind had dropped off to nothing and in the calm we felt quite secure at anchor.

Everything was fine until about three in the morning when the wind picked up and the boat began to dance around. I went on deck to check the anchor and found a strong southeast wind blowing into the bay along with a nasty little chop. I looked around and couldn't make out the Girl Scout Camp.

We weren't anchored where we should be. Instead we were moving rapidly across the bay sideways to the wind. Before I could do anything about it the bowsprit of *Southwind* struck the side of a 40-foot ketch anchored just off the rocks at the far end of the bay. The bobstay snapped like a rotten string. The occupants of the ketch poured out of the cabin just in time to throw a fender between the boats as we scraped down their starboard side. The rocks loomed behind us just a few feet away.

The owner of the ketch proved what a nice guy he was by grabbing our bow line and tying it off to his stern. If he had just pushed us off like he had every right to do, after we rammed his boat and scarred up his topsides, we would have hit the rocks for sure. We didn't have time to try to start the engine which wasn't that reliable anyway.

After we all settled down the owner of the ketch agreed that it would be all right for us to hang there for the rest of the night, and we again went back to get some sleep. The next morning we found that our own anchor had also snugged up pretty well and we were quite comfortable tied to the ketch as well as our own anchor. The wind still blew into the bay and we were still very close to the rocks.

Around noon the ketch decided to head for home but when they tried to start their engine it would not turn over. They called the harbor patrol and requested a tow off the lee shore so they could sail home. The patrol boat was glad to help and we let go of their stern line and hung on our own anchor. The tow boat began its job as they started to hoist their anchor, but the anchor would not budge. It was a big heavy fisherman hook and it had obviously hung up under a rock. The owner of the ketch by this time was quite frustrated and rather then fight the anchor, he pulled the bitter end out of his boat and threw it to us. Then he was towed out to sea and sailed away.

With this anchor and our own, we knew we were well secured and decided to stay a couple more days. We even were able to bum some food from other boats in the bay to supplement our beer and potato chips, which was all we had left. We had a fine couple of days.

When we finally left, I tried to hoist the big anchor and could not budge it. It was down in over 60 feet of water and I could not dive that deep, so I took a knife and diving down as deep as I could, cut the rope and let the rest fall to the bottom. At least I saved the rope. Pulling our own anchor we set sail for home with 200 feet of 3/4 inch nylon coiled on the bow. The trip home was a good sail but I felt guilty about the anchor I had cut. A diver could have retrieved it but I didn't have any money to pay for one.

It was about a month later while driving by Long Beach Marina that I spotted the ketch at its dock. I took the rope and put it in the cockpit with a note of thanks to the owner. At least he got part of his anchor rode back.

There was another incident in Whites Cove that I remember well. I had *Odin* at the time and several members of South Shore Yacht Club had cruised over in a group. We all took up moorings near each other in the bay. Next to me was a member with a Seawolf Ketch, a heavy full keel boat.

About midnight the good old southeast wind blew in again and the Seawolf broke away from its bow mooring. I awoke when it banged heavily against the side of *Odin*. I had to jump on board to wake the owner and tell him his boat was loose.

I think he was suffering from a hangover because he came on deck in a really bad mood. With several swear words he proceeded to crank up the engine and attempted to re-secure the bow mooring line. He knew only full speed ahead or full reverse.

His first attempt to motor forward to the mooring resulted in a tremendous surge ahead which missed the mark. When he put the engine in neutral, the weight and elasticity of the stern mooring dragged him backward and swung him into the boat on the opposite side of the mooring.

He again rammed the throttle into full forward and tearing along the side of our neighbor, ripped off the port shrouds of that boat. This really shook him up and he rammed the gear into reverse and tore away from the boat, pulling out the lifeline stanchions. Here he came again, careening towards me. By this time I had a big fender in my hands and was able to fend off a direct hit on the side of *Odin*. This guy didn't know the meaning of easy does it.

The only thing that saved us from total destruction was that the next time he roared into reverse the stern mooring slacked off and wound around the prop, killing the engine and probably bending the shaft. With the beast tamed, the rest of us, with the help of a dinghy, were able to secure the bow mooring and tie the boat securely for the night.

The next day he had to be towed off his mooring, after a diver cut away the line around his prop. I'll bet the insurance man hated to see him coming.

2

TWIN HARBORS

The next morning was gray with low clouds but no fog. It was cool but not uncomfortable with a light southeast breeze blowing across the cove, just the right direction for sailing up the northeast side of Catalina. Sausage and eggs and a cup of coffee made a quick easy breakfast and by nine o'clock I had raised the main and foresail, and letting go the mooring, silently slipped out from under Long Point and headed west.

It's about seven miles up to the Isthmus and, at the two or three knots the boat was sailing, it was going to take some time. But there is always the engine later on if necessary. I had till about five in the afternoon to make the next mooring.

After clearing Long Point I raised the genoa and main staysail. This gave the boat another knot and in a few minutes I put up the fisherman and sheeted it home. This was fun. I was single-handing with five sails up. With the wind aft of the beam I quickly rigged the square topsail and had it flying. Now the little ship looked good to me, a small tall ship, and I was sailing before the mast.

As we slipped past twin rocks just west of Goat Harbor, I was reminded of a passage made by the family in *Sunlit*. It was a lesson on how not to prepare the kids on what to expect while sailing. We had transited the Panama Canal and moved on to the small resort island of Isla Grande. After a week of leisure at anchor on this beautiful tropical island, we made ready to start the rigorous trip east across the top of South America.

I had studied the charts and read several books about the difficulty of this run. Don Street says in his book, A cruising Guide to The Lesser Antilles, that it is easier to sail westerly around the world to reach the Caribbean than to go east from Panama.

My mistake was in showing my concern to the kids. I had described the tough trip to them and as we departed Isla Grande I warned them to get ready for the problems ahead.

Everything might have gone all right except, just as we headed out from behind the lee of Isla Grande into the wind and rough seas of the Caribbean, the rudder jammed hard over and we started moving in circles with no control and two large rocks (twin rocks) looming just to leeward.

My kids were scarred to death and Heather began to cry uncontrollably. This made it very difficult to figure out how to control the boat, find the rudder problem and prevent the boat from hitting the rocks. It was very disconcerting and even I was shook up.

While Joan tried to calm the kids, I dove into the stern lazarette to try to find the problem. We didn't have much time as the rocks were closer than ever. I had to toss a lot of gear aside to get down to the steering cables.

Fortunately I found the trouble quickly. A bolt had slipped off the auto pilot and prevented the rudder from moving. I cleared the cable and this freed the steering. We were able to straighten out the boat and sail past the rocks into safe water. Once we were under control and on course, it was not too difficult to reattach the auto pilot and put everything back in place.

But let me tell you I came close to panic with the whistling winds, screaming kids and a boat completely out of control for some unknown reason. I didn't realize how terrifying for the young children my description of our trip must have been and I learned that one should be much more careful in telling stories that aren't necessarily true. I now realize how brave those kids were to venture out with us into the unknown.

* * * * * * * * * *

Back on *Iwalani*, I watched the Twin Rocks fade away behind me and began looking forward to finding an anchorage at the Isthmus. Nearing the blue cavern point the Boy Scout square rigged ketch *Argus*, out of Newport, reached in alongside me with its square sails flying.

I have always wanted to sail on a square rigger but never had the chance to ship aboard any of the great tall ships that are found throughout the world. I have been aboard several when they were at dock, and I have sailed along side a few during my cruising experiences. It is always exciting to see a square rigged ship sailing on the open sea.

As *Iwalani* sailed in along side of *Argus*, I was quite happy that I had added those funny spars to the foremast of my little schooner.

LIBERTAD

It was during the cruise on *Sunlit*, while we were moored at the west end of the Panama Canal, that my family and I had the opportunity to see the Argentine Tall Ship *Libertad*. It steamed up the channel opposite our mooring with the crew manning every yard on all three masts. The 338-foot full-rigged ship had four men standing at attention on each yard of the ship - one on each side of the mast and one at the end of each yardarm. The mainmast stood over 300 feet in the air and it made a magnificent sight.

All the yachts moored at the yacht club were blowing horns, cheering and waving. I was so excited that I used up a full canister on the air horn. I even forgot to take pictures. *Libertad* moved on up the canal and tied up to the wharf under the All American Bridge.

The next day the ship held an open house and my family and I went on board for a tour of the ship. We were hosted by two of the over 100 midshipmen on board. After the tour we invited the two midshipmen to join us on our boat. The next day we had the fun of giving them a tour of *Sunlit*.

Later, during the passage from Bimini to Fort Lauderdale, Florida, we sailed alongside the US Coast Guard bark, *Eagle*, for several hours, watching men work the sails and operate the ship. Experiences like these have given me a great love for square-rigged ships.

* * * * * * * * * *

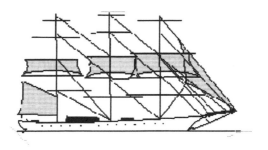

LIBERTAD
A TRUE TALL SHIP

* * * * * * * * * *

Argus had a mooring close into the pier at Twin Harbor and we followed it in and picked up an empty mooring in the center of the bay. I had spotted two familiar boats from San Pedro and looked forward to renewing friendships with some of the gang from the marine industry. They were all experienced sailors, most of them having spent years in boats, cruising all over the world.

I had heard rumors that there might be a party this weekend across the Isthmus at Cat harbor. I had a feeling I could talk them into letting me join in the fun. When they threw a party it was usually pretty good.

A truism crossed my mind. There is a thing about cruising in a sailboat. It is hard to fake it. It may be a cliche, but it is true that the ocean can weed out the fakes and the ill prepared. Don't get me wrong. You don't have to buy out the marine store or own the largest yachts. I have met cruisers who sail the seas in many types of boats, some that might be less then fully seaworthy. It's more a state of mind. The successful ones don't seem to be craving publicity or looking for stardom. They sometimes achieve it, but usually after they have proven themselves and finished the adventure, not at the beginning, telling everybody what a great feat they will perform.

Case in point:

AN AROUND THE WORLD CRUISER

It was about six or seven years ago that he came into Dad's and started to buy items for his boat. He was quite friendly but I really didn't like him very much. It's hard for somebody like myself who thinks he knows all about sailboats to like someone else who knows it all and isn't interested in my opinion at all. Each time he came in he knew exactly what he wanted and would take no advice from me nor could I pin him down on what he was doing.

My curiosity was growing but his attitude showed he had no interest in my opinion and wasn't about to ask for any help. All I did was ring up the sales: anchors, line, EPIRB, blocks, some charts and a sat nav. My curiosity finally got the better of me and I decided to pin down where all this stuff was going. I asked him directly what he had in mind.

"I am going to be the first person to sail around the world non stop," was his answer. OH, OH, I thought, this guy must know something I don't.

"Didn't Robin Knox Johnson already do that?", I asked him.

A sneering smile crossed his face as he answered, "Robin Knox Johnson anchored one night."

"Oh," I decided to humor him and my next question was, "how are you going to do this feat?"

"I am going to Cape Horn and turn left," was a very haughty reply. I decided not to pursue this thing any further but just sell him what he wanted, reaping whatever harvest I could from this great sailor.

I was not the only person who heard of this great feat. There was great to-do and fanfair in the newspapers and TV regarding this non-stop trip around the world. One reporter finally asked him what sailing experience he previously had, and it came out that his total sailing had been about one year on Lake Tahoe in his Westsail 42. However, he, his wife, and his mother-in-law were going to add new records to the annals of sailing. "We are going to Cape Horn and turn left."

Now a Westsail 42 is a well-built boat, but it has a reputation of being a little slow. In fact we used to call them "wet snails." I think It would be very difficult to carry enough food and water for three people nonstop around the world. Can you imagine spending a year, non stop, on a sailboat with your wife and mother-in-law?

Well, it turned out that they got about 200 miles south of Cabo San Lucas and ran into a little weather. They had to abandon ship due to seasickness. After sending out a May Day, they were picked up by a passing freighter. I guess the seas on Lake Tahoe were not the best training for going around the world nonstop.

* * * * * * * * * *

"Oh boy," I thought, as I watched the sun set behind the hill. The goats had wandered back up the trail into the hills and the shadows had crossed the bay. It certainly is easy to laugh at people when their dreams fall apart. But maybe it takes more than just dreams to make a great adventure. There must be some realistic planning. My Westsail 42 customer had the dream and read the books but fell short on the realistic problems to be faced.

FLORIDA OR BUST

But that wasn't the only person I have met who didn't seem to have the proper respect for long distance cruising. In fact the main yard on my brigantine came from another group of beginning sailors who seemed to think long distance sailing is a simple project. They were a friendly family and I was happy to work with them. They took advice on many things and I sold them charts, a radio and a sat nav.

They hadn't done much sailing and I discovered they were members of the Hells Angels motorcycle gang of Northern California. They had bought a 30-foot Atkins double-ended ketch, built in 1928, and the three of them were working hard to get it ready for long distance sailing. The large square-sail yard was not wanted so I grabbed it. New lights and some new rigging brought the boat up to better sailing shape.

They took much of my advice and we were getting along fine. Then they told me of the trip they had planned. They would sail nonstop from Newport to Panama and, after transiting the canal, they would sail nonstop to Florida, where they had jobs waiting for them. They felt they could make this run in less than two months.

Now keep in mind that these people were good customers and getting their boat ready for the cruise would take a lot of money. My stupidity really showed when I made a big point that their planned trip was impossible and, if they wanted to get to Florida, they should put the ketch on a truck and ship it to Florida.

Wow, did they get upset at that suggestion. I almost blew the whole sale. They did not listen when I explained that their boat could only make about 100 miles per day and that it was well over 3000 miles to the Panama Canal. Getting there in 30 days would be very difficult. It would take a week to get through the canal and, frankly, I didn't think they could make the 1000 miles straight up wind to Florida at that time of year at all.

On departure day we had a little party and I made a point of giving them a Mexican Chart Guide, saying, "I know how macho you guys are but if you get too tired, don't be afraid to pull into a Mexican port, even though you insist on a nonstop sail to Panama".

We saw them off with many good wishes and waves and, just to give you an idea of their planning, the last purchase they made that day was a Porta-pottie. Their head had quit working.

They left about noon and the next day one of my customers described an Atkins ketch drifting off Laguna Beach. The ketch had made about 6 miles in a little less than 20 hours after leaving the harbor.

It was two months later that I heard about the finish of the cruise. After 15 days of sailing, the boat was hit by a large wave off Cabo San Lucas and the rudder broke off. They made it into Cabo San Lucas where they also found a large crack in the keel.

They were able to sail to Puerto Vallarte where the boat sat for over a year. I don't know if they ever got those jobs in Florida but I think they were happy to have that Mexican Chart Guide.

STRANGE VESSELS

I remember another adventurer who built a craft and launched it in Newport. It was a large cylinder, a tin can if you will, about 20 feet in diameter with a 10-foot draft and six feet of topsides. On its deck was fashioned the superstructure of a Spanish galleon with masts and a poop deck. 'Tween decks, I understand there was a water bed. The round boat was ballasted to float upright in the water.

The plan was to be towed out into the ocean where they could catch the westward currents and drift to Hawaii. Their first try in the ocean proved a little unsettling because the craft bobbed up and down too much. It made the water bed slosh. To cure this tendency they lowered the center of gravity by attaching a 40 foot chain with a large steel ball and hung it from the bottom.

This cured the problem. I saw the creature out in the water and the large swells of the Pacific just passed it by with little movement of the cylinder.

OK, they were on their way to Hawaii. They were towed several miles out into the ocean and cast adrift. A few days later they drifted in to the 10-fathom mark off Dana Point where their ball and chain held them securely in about 60 feet of water a mile or so off shore. They stayed there a few days until the Coast Guard declared them a hazard to navigation. Again they were towed out and drifted in. After about three or four tries I think they gave up.

However, they were not finished yet. Their next craft was a sailing submarine that floated under water but had mast and sails sticking up. Fortunately, however, before they launched this new vessel the Coast Guard refused to let them sail. The craft still rests behind an industrial building, just off the freeway in Fullerton, California.

* * * * * * * * *

By this time darkness had taken over the cove and I could not make out the beach or the shoreline. Going below, the cabin was warm and snug partly because of the kerosene trawler lamp that again hung from the ceiling after the accident on the trip from Newport. The lamp gave off a soft warm glow in the cabin and gave enough light to jot down more ideas for the book. I was laughing hard as I wrote down notes about many of Dad's customers.

I was still chuckling over the memory of that big cylinder with the Spanish Galleon superstructure. I thought to my self, "I shouldn't laugh at other peoples' dreams. We all need dreams." Then the thought of another round boat left me laughing out loud again as I snuggled into my sleeping bag for the night. I'll tell you about it.

SHARK BAIT

I have met many people who do not seem to have enough respect for the ocean. There is one guy that comes to mind who wasn't a sailor at all. I'll describe him as a bass fisherman.

First let me go back to a week before my encounter with this fisherman. My brother John was in town and he was an avid sailor who also liked to fish. I owned a Cal 20 at the time and invited John for a day sail and a fishing trip in the ocean.

Sailing was good but the fishing was even better. We reached back and forth off the Balboa Pier and caught several large bonito which I planned to take home and smoke. Fish can be a little messy in a small sailboat so we strung them on a line and hung them overboard similar to what a bass fisherman might do with his string of fish.

With six or seven nice tuna we headed for home, dragging the fish along side. Just as we rounded the Newport jetty outer light, the boat was hit with a big slap on her aft quarter. It really bounced the little Cal 20. We never saw what hit us, but when I pulled up the string of fish, all that remained were two heads neatly severed behind the gills. The rest of the large string of fish was gone.

When we inspected the side of the boat, tooth marks were clearly visible in the gelcoat. It seems we were hit by a good sized shark right in the jetty entrance. OK, we know there are big fish out there and I was dumb to drag our fish alongside.

Back to the point of the story. It was a week later when I was returning from a day of sailing that I saw this guy out in the jetty entrance, fishing in one of those double inner tube bass fishing rigs. It was the kind that you sit in a sling in the center with your legs dangling in the water and a small paddle to propel yourself along. Of course any fish you catch are hung on a stringer at your side.

As I sailed by I could not help myself and had to stop and explain to this bass fisherman that he was in danger and suggest that, if he stayed where he was, he could be eaten.

At first he just scoffed at me but when I described the incident of a week earlier at the very spot where he was dangling his feet and his fish, his eyes widened and he started paddling to shore in some haste. Maybe I saved the guy's life.

3

EMERALD COVE

The next day I made the short run up to Emerald Cove and picked up a mooring well inside the bay behind Indian Island. It was only a 30 minute run so I didn't set any sails. Instead I trolled a fishing line and, off Howland's landing, caught a 14-inch Kelp Bass. I had my dinner for the evening. It was not the first time that I have had good luck trolling behind a sail boat.

My thoughts about fishing reminded me of the time Chris, one of my best employees in the store, made a bet with me that he could take me out on *Iwalani* and within an hour catch at least six shark right off Corona Del Mar beach. I thought he was nuts so I took the bet.

On Sundays Dad's Marine closes at three PM. So on the next Sunday, when we closed the store, Chris and I rushed down to *Iwalani* and took off. I steered while Chris mixed up his shark chum and rigged the rods. The chum was a mess of dead fish mixed with peanut butter and other items which I won't mention.

We motored out of the jetty into a nasty chop left over from the day's westerly wind. Not much wind but we sure did rock and roll. In about 10 minutes Chris had spread his chum on the water and, attaching the fishing lines to paper cups, let them drift away from the boat. I thought we might get one fish.

Well, it took about two minutes before the first strike and Chris yanked in a 25-pound blue shark. Seconds later I grabbed the second rod and had my hands full with another big blue. Before I got it in Chris had another shark flapping like mad in the cockpit. In 30 minutes we had caught seven or eight blue shark from 10 to 30 pounds each. Remember this was just 1/4 mile from the Newport entrance.

Needless to say I lost my bet. I also got sick as a dog in the wild chop and bloody fish smell. After half an hour I yelled uncle and headed the boat back to the harbor. Chris made the sad joke that we couldn't have done near as well if I hadn't helped in the chumming. A word to the wise, don't bet against experts.

GREAT WHITE SHARKS

I've had some experience with sharks. I have seen some very big ones in the ocean. I remember seeing one great dorsal fin slip by the side of my boat that stuck three feet up in the air. That fin alone would have fed shark-fin soup to a crew of six for a week.

One time while day dreaming on the bow of the boat I caught a glimpse of a gray shape over twenty feet long slip down under the boat. There are big fish in the sea.

It was on the two-year cruise of *Sunlit* from Newport through the Panama Canal to Florida that I had several contacts with sharks. The most memorable was on the Island of Coiba off the Pacific coast of Panama. We had pulled into a little bay just offshore of an exclusive fishing resort, the Club Pacifica. We had dropped our anchor into about 30 feet of water and settled down for an afternoon lunch.

We planned to go ashore somewhat later. As we ate our sandwiches a sloop flying a German flag sailed in from the south and anchored nearby. After squaring away his boat, the sailor slipped on his snorkel gear and jumped over the side. I presumed he was going after some conch for supper.

His jumping into the water seemed to cause a great commotion from the shore. Two or three of the locals, who had been working on the boats dragged up on shore, started shouting, waving their arms and jumping up and down. I detected a word or two in Spanish such as *Stupido* and *Tanto* (idiot). Something was up.

I jumped into my Zodiac and quickly rowed over to the German boat, just as the diver surfaced. I pointed out the action on the beach and Jack, (I later got to know him very well,) wisely climbed out of the water. I returned to *Sunlit* and gathered up the family to go ashore and find out why all the commotion.

As we reached the shore, one of the locals came up to us and, speaking excitedly in Spanish, warned us of the danger of swimming in the bay. Just a few hours earlier a Great White shark had been sighted right where we were anchored. He explained that the resort was a fishing resort and they had a habit of throwing fish remains in the bay, right off the beach in front of us.

"Come, come," they shouted, "we will show you some pictures. This is what we caught a week ago," and he held up a picture of a monstrous White shark.

"See that barge out there." He was pointing at a small flatbed barge anchored near our boat. It was used to ferry their provision truck over from the mainland.

"We had a small chunk of beef which we attached to a shark hook on a rope. Then we hung it off the barge over night. The next morning the barge was bobbing up and down so we went out to see what we caught. We began pulling in a medium-sized shark of about 400 pounds. We had it almost to the edge of the barge when from underneath came this monster and swallowed our 400 pound shark whole.

"We were now attached to a Great White shark weighing about 2000 pounds. It took a good fight but we landed it and, after killing it, we hung the shark up on that fish tower over there," and he pointed to the hoist where marlin and other big fish are hoisted up to be photographed.

"We all were taking pictures, here, look at these", and he stuffed a batch in my hand. "We wanted the fish to look ferocious so somebody pulled its jaws open. Out fell the 400-pound Lemon shark and right behind it came a 300-pound sea turtle." He pointed at the pictures to verify the story, "a big fish, no??"

"A big fish, yes," I said, gazing at the pictures.

"Then," my friend went on to say, "we cut out its jaws and went to set them out to dry on a fifty gallon drum. They slipped right over the drum and could have swallowed that too."

"You must be careful where you swim in these waters."

Our visit to Coiba Island was fascinating and we later did a considerable amount of diving--a long way from the fishing camp in waters we were told would be much safer.

Those were big fish off Panama. But let me tell you of a creature much closer to home that came very close to sinking the boat I was on.

I'LL TELL YOU A TALE
A WHALE OF A TALE
A TALE OF A WHALE
I HAVE TO TELL

"This is real sailing," yelled Jack, the owner and skipper of *Swift*, a Newport 41 sloop that I have crewed on for many years. The Ensenada race was on. Our start was good at the weather end of the line and the wind was out of the southwest on our beam at about 8 knots. "Let's get the chute up," came the order from the skipper, who steered the boat from the leeward aft cockpit. He leaned far over gazing around the genoa.

"Aye sir," the reply came from the rest of us on the crew and the action that looked like chaos was really well practiced teamwork by experienced sailors. The pole was lifted, sheets and afterguys tightened and within seconds the red, white and blue spinnaker blossomed into its full beauty from the foredeck of the boat. *Swift* leaped ahead and we settled down to get the best speed out of her for the rest of the afternoon.

The six of us on board were all experienced hands and could get the most out of this well-equipped racing boat. We had sailed together on many races, Jack, Dave, Howie, Rennie, Don and myself, a friendly and hard-working bunch of sailors.

By sunset the wind had carried us well down the coast past Oceanside and we felt we were doing well in our class. After dark the offshore winds filled in as we had expected and we were well past the lee of the

43

South Coronado Island at sunrise. By 8 o'clock we were drifting along in zero knots of wind off Rosarito Beach, a mile or so off shore. I was off watch, lying in the starboard quarter berth, not quite asleep, listening to Howie bagging his zz's in the port berth.

"Look out!!", came a cry. Crash, came a great sound off the hull. "What the hell was that?" Jack yelled from the deck. I was out of my hole and into the cabin in a second. I gazed up at Dave on the wheel in time to have a large blast of water hit me in the face. Dave's eyes were as large as saucers while he stood there clinging to the wheel.

"Have we run aground?", I shouted, but a quick look out the porthole proved that was wrong. Shore was a long way off. Then, as I watched Dave, the wheel spun from his hands and turned wildly to starboard. Dave was tossed against the side of the cockpit.

Then the boat surged upward, lifted by a great hand and toppled to its side crashing down into the sea. A wall of water fell onto the deck. As I scrambled up the ladder I was met with another wash of water as a giant tail flipped in my face and disappeared into the ocean depths.

"Are we sinking?" Jack yelled, and I dashed below and yanked up the floorboards. "No water coming in here," I screamed back, "we seem OK."

"I've got no steering", Dave said from the wheel as he gave it a spin and it continued to rotate with no force at all.

44

"OK, guys settle down", came Jack's reassuring voice. "Lets check the damage and see what's wrong."

"Dave, keep steering with the sails, ease the main out and tighten the jib."

"Bill, let me by to check the steering cables." And I squeezed aside as he started pulling loose the companion ladder and tossing aside the gear stowed behind it.

"There is our problem," he said in a calmer voice as he showed me the broken steering cable and pointed out the bent bronze sheaves that carried the gear.

"It looks as if the rudder is still there," yelled Howie from the aft deck where he hung over the side peering down under the stern. "It seems bent but still in place."

"We have work to do," said Jack. "I will need a hammer, some wire clamps and wrenches." I pulled open the well-stocked tool drawer and was able to hand Jack all he asked for as he lay on the bilge with his head sticking under the cockpit floor. He soon tossed me a wire sheave. It had been sawed through by the wire as it was stripped by the force of the rudder slammed hard over.

I was able to straighten it out with a few blows of the hammer; this gave it a serviceable appearance. Jack took the hammer and with a few swings was able to straighten the bracket that held the sheave.

"This will take a while but we can do it," Jack reported, and in about an hour we rove the wire, clamped it tight and had the steering working again.

"It looks as if our trophy hopes have been bashed," Howie went on excitedly.

"Pardon the pun. What the hell happened?"

"It was a whale," Dave replied. "A really mad whale. I saw him coming just before he hit the side. Then he spun past our stern and hit us straight on from the back, ripping the wheel out of my grasp. After that he dove underneath us and rose up about 6 feet and dumped us on our side. I was scared." It was an understatement.

"I got on deck just in time to see him flip his tail at us and fill the cockpit with water," I said, to put in my two-bits worth.

No one else had a good look at the whale but we all agreed that it was one mad beast. It was about 50 feet long and it certainly weighed more than our boat. Later a report from a nearby racing boat described the scene much the same. The crew stared in wonderment at the geysers of water around our boat as we were buffeted and bounced by the whale.

We finished the race but of course the hour or so lost in fixing the rudder killed our chances of winning any trophies. However, we did have a lot to talk about around the Bahia bar.

The boat was dented but did not break. A wooden hull or a less sturdy fiberglass hull would most likely have been holed and sunk. This is the one time in my life that I felt I was a true survivor.

4

CAT HARBOR

On Saturday morning the sky was gray and a cool north wind blew across the harbor. It was going to be a beat out of Emerald and up to the west end of Catalina.

With the Perkins purring away, I let go the mooring and motored out around Indian Island. When I was free of the rocks, I went forward and raised the main and forestaysail. These two sails along with the engine would take me around the West End of Catalina. The next hour of heavy beating would clean *Iwalani's* decks very nicely.

* * * * * * * * * *

I remember a race several years ago when I didn't make it around the West End. It was a race from San Pedro, around Catalina, to Newport. I was sailing my Ericson 32, *Odin*, with a crew of four including my son, Ross.

We had a good sail across the Catalina Channel but as we neared the West End the wind was up to well over 35 knots and the seas had built up to a hard steep swell with a heavy chop on top. We were down to our smallest jib and a reefed main.

47

My son had slipped on the cabin floor and hurt his arm. It was not broken but he was in pain. However, we felt we were doing well so we were pushing the boat hard in increasingly heavy weather. We were thinking of the possibility of a trophy and we didn't like quitting.

Approaching the West End we tacked short of the cliffs. Seeing the water dashing on the rocks was quite foreboding. After about 5 minutes on port tack we were getting ready to make our final turn to round the West End Rock.

Somebody on board made the comment that if we passed those rocks we were going to have to spend the whole night out there in what was getting more and more miserable. It was getting dark and there were no safe harbors for the next 30 miles.

Were we ready for a rough night in 35 to 40-knot winds, running in what could be survival conditions? The decision was easy. No!

It took just a few seconds to put the tiller to windward and head the boat off the wind. We had just one tricky maneuver and that was to jibe in the heavy wind and swells. Hanging on for dear life we bought the boat around. As we all ducked down the main slammed over. The boat lay on its side but nothing broke and now we were on a nice safe quartering reach heading for Arrow Point and the lee of the island.

It took only about ten minutes before we made the lee and calm water. A few minutes later we picked up a mooring in the western corner of the Isthmus. As we battened down the boat, a Lapworth 48 IOR racer took up a mooring near by; her mast laying in pieces on the deck.

Later we learned of three other boats that had serious trouble. One ran aground on the island and another lost its rudder and had to be towed in by the Coast Guard in a sinking condition, with water rushing in through the hole where the rudder post had been.

The next morning when we inspected our boat we had the cleanest decks ever. Salt water had scoured every trace of dirt.

* * * * * * * * * *

This time I was going to make it around the point. It was rough but not a real storm. Just typical May weather for the windward side of Catalina. The spray was flying and a green wave or two did wash over the deck. It was blowing about 25 knots.

For *Iwalani* these conditions were not severe. Under main, forestaysail and the diesel turning at about fifteen hundred RPM, *Iwalani* could make about 4 knots and not shake the boat up too much. I wanted to make that picnic at Cat Harbor in the afternoon.

With the West End Rock laying on our port quarter I turned the boat downwind and eased the sheets. Running in following seas. Boat speed was up to about six knots. I was going to make the party.

* * * * * * * * * *

Sailing in these conditions reminded me of another great downwind run I made many years ago. It was a spring race around Santa Barbara Island aboard an Olson 35 yawl. It was one of the first ocean races I had been able to crew on and, to be frank, the beat from San Pedro to Santa Barbara was not much fun.

I tend to get seasick when beating hard to weather and this race was no exception. I think it was this race that gave me a reputation as the best green foredeck man in the fleet. Even while sick I usually am able to get my job done and race hard. Just keep the lee rail clear.

We rounded the island late at night and by mid-morning we were running downwind with full main, spinnaker, mizzen and mizzen staysail. All the sail we could carry. It was my turn at the tiller and I loved it. I am a pretty good helmsman especially off the wind. To control a well-balanced boat under lots of sail is a real thrill.

The boat would poise on the top of a swell and then pick up speed as we rushed down the front side keeping pace with the large swells. The game was to peg the speedometer and see how long we could hold it there. The knotmeter registered to 11 knots and the longest I could keep the needle pegged was over 10 seconds as we rushed along at probably 15 knots. Then we would drop off the wave and have to wait for the next one.

I was doing a pretty good job of keeping up the boat speed up, so the rest of the crew did not force me to leave the tiller when the watch was up. I steered that boat for over 3 hours and relished all of it. It wasn't until the wind eased and boat speed dropped off the peg that I grew tired and was relieved of the tiller. I didn't have a twinge of seasickness on that downwind run.

* * * * * * * * * *

Rounding Catalina Head and slipping into the lee I headed up wind and lowered the sails. Five minutes later *Iwalani* was well up into the bay and I dropped anchor just off the beach where the picnic was going strong. I received many waves from the crowd and that night the sea chanteys rung loud into the darkness.

I have always enjoyed Catalina parties. They are a lot of fun. There usually is a good guitar player somewhere in the crowd and to sit around a camp fire singing sea chanteys is a real part of sailing and cruising. "Blow the Man Down," "the Eddystone Light" and "Hoist up the John B Sail" all sound even greater when you can turn and gaze out at your own ship anchored in the bay.

The singing lasted well into the evening. There was steak and salad for everyone and a keg of beer decorated the picnic bench. There was also a bottle or two passed around. Luckily no one was driving this night, however, we did watch each other carefully as we dinghyed back to our boats. Everybody made it safely. I was still humming a few tunes as I slipped into the sleeping bag.

DRUNKEN SAILOR

WAY HEY AND UP SHE RISES
WAY HEY AND UP SHE RISES
WAY HEY AND UP SHE RISES
EARLYE IN THE MORNING

WHAT DO YOU DO WITH A DRUNKEN SAILOR
WHAT DO YOU DO WITH A DRUNKEN SAILOR
WHAT DO YOU DO WITH A DRUNKEN SAILOR
EARLYE IN THE MORNING

WAY HEY AND UP SHE RISES
WAY HEY AND UP SHE RISES
WAY HEY AND UP SHE RISES
EARLYE IN THE MORNING

PUT HIM IN THE LONG BOAT TILL HE'S SOBER
PUT HIM IN THE LONG BOAT TILL HE'S SOBER
PUT HIM IN THE LONG BOAT TILL HE'S SOBER
EARLYE IN THE MORNING

TRICE HIM UP IN A RUNNING BOWLINE.
TIE HIM TO THE TAFFRAIL WHEN SHE'S YARD ARM UNDER.
PUT HIM IN THE SCUPPERS WITH A HOSE PIPE ON HIM.

WAY HEY AND UP SHE RISES
WAY HEY AND UP SHE RISES
WAY HEY AND UP SHE RISES
EARLYE IN THE MORNING

HAUL AWAY JOE

WAY HAUL AWAY, WE'LL HAUL FOR BETTER WEATHER
WAY HAUL AWAY, WE'LL HAUL, AWAY JOE
WAY HAUL AWAY, WE'LL HAUL AWAY TOGETHER
WAY HAUL AWAY, WE'LL HAUL, AWAY JOE

NOW WHEN I WAS A LITTLE BOY
AN' SO ME MOTHER TOLD ME,
THAT IF I DIDN'T KISS THE GALS
MY LIPS WOULD GET ALL MOULDY

WAY HAUL AWAY, WE'LL HAUL FOR BETTER WEATHER
WAY HAUL AWAY, WE'LL HAUL, AWAY JOE

AND I SAILED THE SEAS FOR MANY A YEAR
NOT KNOWING WHAT I WAS MISSING
THEN I SET ME SAILS AFORE
THE GALES AND STARTED IN A KISSING

WAY HAUL AWAY, WE'LL HAUL FOR BETTER WEATHER
WAY HAUL AWAY, WE'LL HAUL, AWAY JOE

EDDYSTONE LIGHT

MY FATHER WAS THE KEEPER OF THE EDDYSTONE LIGHT
AND HE SLEPT WITH A MERMAID ONE FINE NIGHT
AND FROM THIS UNION THERE CAME THREE
A PORPOISE AND A WHALE AND THE OTHER WAS ME

YO HO HO AND THE WIND BLOWS FREE

55

A CUNA INDIAN DANCE PARTY

Let me tell you of another great party. The kind you find in the pages of the National Geographic Magazine. It was on the island of Plyon Chico in the San Blas Islands of Panama.

We had anchored in a little bay called Hidden Harbor, an uninhabited island about half way into the San Blas Island chain. We were just settling in when an Indian dugout canoe with a small man and four children paddled up and introduced themselves. We invited them aboard for a snack.

Charley Smith was the elderly man's name and the children were his grand kids. They ranged from about four to six years of age. They were very polite and seemed to enjoy being aboard our boat. They certainly enjoyed the snacks we provided.

Charley told us that he wanted to be our guide and that we must come over to Plyon Chico for their grand festival which was to begin in two days. People from all over the islands were coming and there would be parades, a basketball tournament and dance contests. The festival would last almost a week.

We agreed to sail over to the town the next day and Charley promised he would meet us and show us a good anchorage. Charley was an extraordinary man. He was about 70 years old and spoke seven languages, a Cuna Indian who had worked on freighters around the world, and upon retirement had returned to his native San Blas Islands where he was greatly respected by his fellow villagers. He had six children and at least 14 grandchildren, the newest being about three weeks old. We were introduced to the whole family.

The next two days were spent watching parades and the basketball tournament. The islanders really played good ball. I was amazed at their shooting accuracy and moves on the court. I made the comment that they could play against some of the good college teams in the states. Then my wife Joan walked across the court and she stood at least a head taller then their biggest man. She is five feet six inches tall.

The highlight of the week was our invitation to watch the dance contest that evening. This turned out to be a great party. We gathered in the center of the village under Colman gas lanterns. The village elders sat in a VIP area overlooking the dance floor. Charley introduced us to the group and we settled in to watch some extraodinary dancers from several nearby islands

There were four groups of eight dancers, four men and four women per group. They danced a kind of square dance. Each man played a pan-style reed flute and the women shook rhythm tambourines. The music was exotic, loud and very rhythmic. The object was to go as fast and as long as possible.

The dancing had been going on for almost an hour when Charley came over to me and pointing at my Polaroid camera, which I had kept out of sight, insisted I take a picture of the group.

I have often heard that the San Blas people did not want their pictures taken and even the old myth about steeling their soul with a camera had been mentioned, so I did not want to start something with a flash camera.

Charley kept insisting and would poke his elbow into my side, urging me to take some pictures. About then I had a brilliant idea. I handed Charley the camera and told him to take the picture.

Amazing things began to happen. Charley took the camera and immediately moved over to the VIP section in front of the elders. Charley was, with out a doubt, a showman. Have you ever seen someone with a camera who is very slow in taking a picture. Charley stood with the camera at his eye and his hand on the shutter button. All the dancers were watching him as they continued their dancing at full speed.

He stood there for almost a full minute while the dancers kept going. Then he tripped the shutter and the flash illuminated the whole area.

All hell broke loose. The dancers rushed to surround Charley. They grabbed the picture as it was ejected from the camera. Everyone wanted to see it and then everyone wanted to have their picture taken.

The flash camera was passed around and pictures were snapped almost as fast as the camera could spit out the picture. It wasn't long before it was out of film and the people came to me to ask for more film. I had another role and quickly refilled the camera and it was off on another round. The pictures were passed all around the square. Dancing was completely halted and even the elders wanted their pictures taken. It was hectic.

I don't think anybody ever won the dance contest

and I never got my hands on any of the pictures. They all disappeared into the crowd.. When the film was gone they gave me back the empty camera. What a night. My flash camera completly stole the dancing show but the people loved it. And I don't think I stole a single soul.

THE GREEN FLASH,
MOON BOWS, AND LIGHTNING

I have seen the GREEN FLASH! There really is such a phenomenon and I've seen it.

All my life, every time I have watched an ocean sunset, I've looked for it. It is an excuse to sip a little toddy and gam with the crew. It has become a ritual with me whenever I am at sea.

For many years I had thought of it as just a myth and a good excuse to relax for a few minutes to gaze at nature's beauty. I never had seen the green flash but never gave up hope that it was real.

Well, it is. I've only seen it once but I know it's there. It was on our run from the Isla Testigos to Grenada in the southern West Indies. We were just settling down for a slow night heading north. We had gathered in the cockpit before the evening meal and the change of watch. As the sun dipped below the horizon the instant flash of green was clearly visible. I really saw it. And I won't forget it.

What! You don't know of the green flash? Let me tell you what it is. First you need a clear view of the horizon, no land in the way. You also need exceptionally clean air with no fog or mist. As the sun sets the light rays pass through the Earth's atmosphere. An instant after the upper limb of the sun drops below the horizon the green area of the light spectrum flashes across the horizon. A rare sight indeed.

Hey, there is another phenomenon out there that I have seen. A rainbow made by the moon. A Moonbow. Now there is an ethereal sight. I've only seen it once, and I had never heard of it before.

It occurred on my second race around Guadalupe Island. We had rounded the island the day before. We had learned of our position from the little Navigator Bird early in the day. It was about two in the morning. The weather was rough and we had been hit by lightning, (I'll describe that experience next).

It had been raining and cloudy but the clouds had cleared very quickly in the north quadrant. The full moon dodged out from behind the fading clouds. It was very bright from the moonlight and there it was: a full half circle of silvery veiled light from horizon to horizon, a rainbow with no color at all. If you ever get to see such a phenomenon it will send a shiver down your spine.

The races I have participated in around Guadalupe Island, which lies about 300 miles south of Newport and 150 miles off the Baja coast of Mexico, have been the source of many of the tales for this book. Sailing on *Swift* is often an adventure, and sailing off the Baja coast can be exciting and unforgettable.

As I have just described, a moonbow is exotic. However, getting hit by lightning is both exotic and considerably more frightening. As I told you earlier, the weather was rough and windy, with rain squalls bearing down on us from the northwest. It was a hard beat under reefed main and small jib with a lot of water on deck.

Of the six of us in the crew only two were on deck. I sat in the companionway in comparative comfort while still on watch. There were lightning strikes every now and then on the horizon. Jack, our skipper, was reclining on the settee trying to relax.

His cry of "let go of the wheel!!" jarred me awake and, as I looked into the cabin, a dancing glow of blue- green light lit the area. Then the lightning hit. The bolt jumped from the top of the mast to the sky in a reverse of what one expects from lightning.

Jack had felt it coming and knew enough to yell for the helmsman to release the stainless steel wheel, thus avoiding any current running through his body. No one was injured but hair stood straight up all around. The radio was fried and the smell of burnt metal pervaded the cabin.

We later found the sailing wind instruments also fried. The lightning bolt had built up in the boat and discharged up the mast into the rain squall above us. Awesome. It was later, after squaring away the damage, that the Moonbow showed us the way towards Newport and calmed our feelings. A night to remember.

* * * * * * * * * *

I think the green flash came to my mind because this really was a morning after. The party last night was probably a little more fun than I'm used to. I had a good old fashioned hangover from the few glasses of beer and maybe a shot or two of rum. Lightning bolts, Moonbows and the Green Flash seemed to fit the state of my head.

One of the fellows at the party was a great guitar player and knew all the old sea chanteys. I even joined in with my concertina. It was one of those rollicking nights that put a party at Catalina on top of the list of happenings.

5

LITTLE HARBOR

It wasn't till about two in the afternoon that I let go the mooring, drifted out of Cat Harbor and headed for Little Harbor, half way down the backside of Catalina. Today the afternoon westerly had already filled in. I didn't set the mainsail at all. The genoa and the two square sails were perfect for this short downwind leg. I didn't feel like fighting with big sails anyway so this made a perfect combination.

It took about an hour and a half to make the 5-mile run down the shoreline. When I got just off the rocks that form a natural jetty for the bay, I dropped the genoa and took down the square sails. The motor brought me into the bay and I anchored in about 10 feet of water well inside the rocky outcropping.

Little Harbor is a well-protected bay when the tide does not get too high. The natural jetty is normally above water except at high tide. Then the rocks submerge, and the Pacific swell rolls right into the bay. It is only on a spring tide that the bay can become too uncomfortable to spend the night. On less high tides it is fine. Also the bay is shallow and if you anchor in close at high tide you might find yourself high and dry 6 hours later. Another reason to watch those spring tides.

It was Monday afternoon and the harbor was empty. I anchored the boat bow out with about a five to one scope. Then I led a stern anchor shoreward with the dinghy and snugged it up tight. Any swells coming in that evening would be bow on and not rock the boat too much. *Iwalani*, being a heavy full-keeled boat, doesn't move too much anyway and I knew I would be quite comfortable.

As the sun set I decided that coffee would be the best for me and a steaming cup kept my hands warm as I watched the sun drop over the horizon. No green flash tonight. But I was feeling better than I did this morning.

* * * * * * * * * *

It was time to do some more work on the book. There are several little stories I would like to relate to my readers that might be interesting. First let me tell you about the Navigator Birds of Guadalupe Island.

Mother Carry's Chickens, the name given by sailors to small sea birds (*Procellaria pelagica*), the presence of which near a ship was supposed to indicate the approach of a storm. The name Mother Cary derives from latin Mater Cara whose birds--*Aves Sanctae Mariae*-- they were supposed to be. French sailors call them *Les oiseaux de Notre Dame*. The bird is ordinarily known as the Storm Petrel, a corruption of the Italian Petrello or little Peter, a name bestowed on it because of its ability to run lightly over the surface of the sea, thus imitating St Peter's achievment to walk on water.

From: "The Oxford Companion to Ships and the Sea"

NAVIGATOR BIRDS

I'm not a superstitious man, nor do I believe in the occult. I have only had one or two experiences in my lifetime that make me wonder about those things.

It was the Navigator Bird of Guadalupe Island that made me wonder the most. I was aboard the 41-foot sloop, *Swift*, on the Around Guadalupe from Newport Race.

We had rounded the island the day before and were on the long beat back to Newport. The weather was bad with 25 knots of wind and fog. By noon we were wondering where the Baja coast might be. Our dead reckoning line on the chart had begun to cross the sands of the beach and soon would be climbing Mount Sierra. We obviously weren't on that line as the waves were still high with no land in sight. I was beginning to wonder about our skipper's navigation. He obviously had overestimated our speed. We didn't know where we were.

During the day, starting about noon, we were visited by those lovely little wonders of the ocean, Mother Carey's Chickens. These are a motley bunch of small birds that seem to have no business miles at sea in such rough weather. They come in a multitude of colors and sizes from small sparrows to robin size.

They seem fearless and will crawl right up your sleeve for a bite of bread. We had several flitting about the boat on this afternoon. While I was down in the cabin discussing our position with the skipper, one little bird seemed very interested in our discussion. It flitted around inside the cabin and seemed to listen to our conversation regarding our dead-reckoning position. We had marked it on the chart as being about 3 miles inland on top of a four thousand foot mountain. Obviously we didn't have a good idea where we were. After our discussion the skipper went on deck and I, being off watch, sat back on the settee and relaxed.

The chart table was abandoned with the chart spread out flat. As I watched, our little bird flitted over to the chart. First it walked to the side of the chart, the latitude edge, and pecked at the edge. Than over to the top edge, the longitude scale, and again pecked at the edge. And as I watched, it moved over to the middle of the chart, wiggled its wings, shook its feathers and left a nice little spot on the chart. Having left its mark, it flew out the hatch and off across the vast ocean.

The clock struck 4 bells and it was time to change the watch. It wasn't until 3 hours later that we got a good fix on the Mexican coast. Tracing the fix backwards we discovered that the bird had left its mark on the exact position of our boat at the time. It knew where it was and was eager to show us the way. I won't try to convince anybody, but I know that little bird had our best interests in mind. Maybe it was the spirit of Cabrillo haunting those waters. Or Saint Peter himself watching over our progress.

* * * * * * * * * *

It's nice to have little birds do your navigating for you, and it is a good idea to take advantage of every source of information available, but navigation is a serious business. Let me tell you of some of my navigation methods. I have a few important ideas for passage making.

When I cruised down the Mexican coast, I made the decision on overnight passages to always angle offshore during the night and near dawn sail back toward shore again. I felt about a 10 degree or 15 degree offshore course from the base line would guarantee that I would not be swept by currents towards shore.

Near dawn, heading in again, put me in sight of shore after sunrise, and during the day we could skirt the shoreline in safety. This worked very well for me on cruises down the west coast of North America.

Another rule I have always tried to follow is to never enter an unknown harbor or anchorage in the dark. I always tried to plan my passages to be sure I would arrive near dangerous areas or new harbors in daylight. Several times I have made a point of heaving to in darkness so that I would arrive in daylight. It might slow you down a little but it certainly is safer.

Let me tell you of one of my great navigation feats in which I used most of the above tenets. It was a passage I made on *Sunlit* along the top of South America from Scotsman's Cove in Venezuela towards a series of islands and bays about 40 miles further on.

It was an overnight passage and I set the course to be free of any dangers during darkness. The next morning there was nothing in sight ahead of us. Mountains were visible on our starboard side and to port an island was visible. In checking the chart I decided that the island to port was our destination and turned to close the island. I didn't feel it could be too far away. As currents are erratic in this area I didn't trust my dead reckoning.

The boat did not make the headway toward the island that I expected and all day we sailed towards the land on the horizon. I believed we were bucking a current and that was what was slowing us down. I cranked the RPMs of the engine a little higher and continued on.

The course drawn on the chart showed us coming in under the lee of a small uninhabited island where I planned to anchor for the night under the first point. The next three days would be a leisurely cruise through these islands off the coast of Venezuela.

It was just dusk when we pulled in under the western-most point of land and anchored in a quiet open bay for the night. I breathed a sigh of relief because if we had been much later we would have had to turn about and heave to for the night because we would not approach an unknown shore in darkness.

I knew where we were and I pointed out our position on the chart, the bay we were in, and even the little islet off to port was on the map. Because the island was small with no habitation we didn't plan to go ashore. I then described to my family the plans for the next three days of cruising these Venezuelan islands.

That evening my confidence began to unravel. Automobile headlights showed us a busy street just a little way inland. The glow of a city showed just around the point where the chart showed water. Something didn't fit.

The next morning we raised anchor and began our planned three day cruise through the small group of islands. I told the kids that after we rounded the point a passage would open up past the little island and would give way to a long bay leading towards the next group of islands.

Rounding the first point, the island did not give way. Instead the shoreline carried on into a large bay where there should have been nothing but water. Ships were anchored and a ferry boat crossed ahead of us. A large town appeared on the shore of this uninhabited island.

We weren't where we thought we were. My wife suggested we approach one of the anchored ships and ask where we were. I wasn't about to do that. Instead I motored in to an anchorage area of other yachts, set the hook and when we were secure, gathered the family into the dinghy and rowed ashore. We went into the nearest bar and asked where we were. A brilliant navigator's ploy.

It turned out we were about 40 miles from my reckoning. Instead of a leisurely cruise through the small islands, we had knocked about three days off our trip. We were on Margarita Island 40 miles further along our planned course. Now that's fine navigating. Like I said a navigator must use all the resources available to him, even the nearest bar.

A SERIOUS PASSAGE

There was a time when my navigational skill with the sextant did help me a great deal. It was on the passage from Puerto Plata, in the Dominican Republic, to the Turks and Caicos Islands in the south end of the Bahama chain.

It is an overnight passage in rough waters and the Caicos Islands are low and rocky, not easy to find from a distance. Our course to South Caicos was up a 20-mile wide, deep passage between shallow banks edged with small islands and rocks.

We left Puerto Plata at sunset to guarantee we would not approach these islands till well after daylight. The wind was on our back at about 30 knots and the seas were high. It was a dead run and not too uncomfortable. I aimed for the center of the deep water passage. About ten o'clock the next morning we suddenly could see bottom beneath us and we knew we had missed the deep water passage and were coming up on the banks.

One of the beauties of the Bahamas is the clarity of the water. It is often described as clear as gin. Navigation by the color of the water is common in the area.

Rocks lay ahead and the following wind and seas were pushing us towards a lee shore. Where were we? I knew we had to make a turn to reach deep water, but on which side of the passage were we? Do we turn right or left? A mistake could be dangerous and at the very least make it hard to find a safe anchorage.

I decided that if I could get a good sextant sight I could get some idea of which side of the passage we were on. I made several sights in the rough conditions and hurried below to figure them out while the rest of the crew turned the boat to windward to beat out of the shallow water.

It took about 15 minutes, and a trip to the lee rail of the boat to barf because of the rough seas, before I was able to determine that we were west of the passage and had to turn to starboard to regain deep water.

We reached off to the west and an hour later the sand gave way to the dark blue Caribbean under our keel and we were again able to head north towards our destination. In an hour we slipped into Cockburn Harbor and anchored off the Admiralty Arms Inn on South Caicos Island.

This was the one time on my cruise aboard *Sunlit* that I felt we were in serious trouble. If we had come up on the banks in the dark we probably would have sailed right up on the rocks. If we hadn't made those sights we would not have known which way to turn. It pays to know a little celestial navigation.

Now days, of course, every one would have GPS and Loran. But keep in mind that these electronic toys can break. On the cruise of the *Sunlit* we didn't have many navigational tools. The knotmeter broke before we reached Panama and the radio direction finder never seemed to work well in South American waters.

I did learn however, that I could probably sail *Sunlit* around the world figuring her speed at five knots upwind and six knots downwind. My dead reckoning on that trip proved to be very accurate.

73

Maybe it was just luck but I remember a passage across the Great Bahama Bank of the Bahamas. We entered the bank at the Northwest Passage light and steered toward Gun Key which had one of the few openings to deep water on the western side near Bimini Island, which was our destination. At Gun Key we would gain deep water and then sail north to Bimini.

The banks average less then 10 feet deep with many shallow areas less then six feet. *Sunlit* drew just under six feet. There is a passage across but it is necessary to sail from Northwest Passage Light Tower to the Russel Light Tower and then a 35 mile run to the Silvia Beacon Tower near Gun Key. The islands are so low they offer no visual landmarks to use as a fix.

We entered the bank about seven in the morning and picked up the Russel tower right on schedule. From there it was almost straight west to the Silvia Beacon. We sailed in company of another boat that was following our same course.

As we headed west we gradually moved ahead of the other boat but we were able to hear him on the radio talking to someone in Bimini. Right on time and almost where it was supposed to be we came upon a tower sticking out of the water and I was sure it was the Silvia Beacon. The problem was that the light was not working and there would be no way to see it at night. If we had missed the tower, it would have been hard to get a fix.

About 3:45 in the afternoon using Silvia as a point of departure, we changed course for the 10-mile run to Gun Key. I radioed the boat behind us that I had found the beacon and he should be able to see it in a few minutes as I was sure he was only a mile or so behind us.

We then sailed on to Gun Key arriving before dark and anchored just inside the passage off the banks. Listening to the radio I learned that the boat behind us had not spotted the Silvia tower and was still out searching for it. He was kind of in a panic and did not know which way to go.

The next morning listening to the radio I discovered that he had anchored on the bank and still hadn't figured out where he was. I had no idea how to direct him off the bank and often wonder how he found his way. At the time I didn't realize it but I was very lucky to find my way.

* * * * * * * * * *

It was a very comfortable night at Little Harbor, in the peace and quite of the backside of Catalina. And I had a fine night's sleep, although I did stay up quite late working on this book. The next morning I was up early and took my 9-foot rubber dinghy to shore to have a little walk along the only open surfing beach on Catalina. It lies just south east of the anchorage.

Little Harbor also has a shoreside campsite and it gave me a chance to deposit a bag of trash in the cans on the beach. As a believer in clean water I don't throw trash overboard. Catalina does a good job of keeping their shoreline clean.

75

A MEAN PELICAN

On the cruise aboard *Sunlit* we always bagged our trash and stored it on the after deck for disposal at the next port. This sometime caused a few problems.

In the tropics if you leave garbage out very long it gets a little ripe and can attract odd creatures. On one occasion while we were anchored in the Isla Testigos of Venezuela, I arose late at night to check the deck and was startled at hearing a strange sound coming from the stern.

Turning on a flashlight, I illuminated a very large pelican helping himself to the garbage. It had ripped open the bag and had its contents scattered all over. I took a handy boat hook and made some motions to scare the medieval beast away.

Now I think the pelican is the dumbest bird there is. This one was no different except it was a trained sword fighter. Every time I tried to force him off the boat he parried my thrusts with his beak. He would not leave. The bird even grew bolder and started to attack me. I was on the defensive and had to parry the long thrusts of his large beak. With 6 foot wings flapping he was formidable indeed and I retreated to rethink the problem.

I decided I needed reinforcements and woke my wife to join me on deck. She armed herself with a broom and while I distracted the bird with the boat hook, a well-placed swing with the broom forced the pelican over the side where it flapped off into the darkness with a mighty squawk.

I'll tell you it certainly left a mess. Not only was the garbage spread all over but pelican droppings painted the whole stern deck white and required a long morning with soap, mop and buckets of water to clean it up.

These are the costs of trying to keep the world clean.

ALWAYS BAG YOUR GARBAGE

It was further up the West Indies chain that we had a good laugh over our efforts to keep the oceans clean. We had two large garbage bags full of trash on the stern and planned to dispose of them on our next port of call, St. Barts Island. Our efforts at ecology gave us a kind of smug feeling of true environmentalists.

As we rounded the southern point of St. Barts Island we saw a trash truck climbing a hill from the beach. We knew it was heading for a trash fill further up the island. We were wrong. The truck crawled along the cliff side keeping pace with our course along the shore. We watched as the truck came to a long cement ramp hanging over the cliff. It backed up to the ramp and raising the dump truck bed, dropped its load of garbage and trash onto the ramp and we watched the load slide down into the sea.

We made the decision at once to save the islanders the cost of transporting our two bags of garbage, and deposited them into the center of the floating mess as we sailed by.

KEEP YOUR POWDER DRY

As I rowed out from the shore at Little Harbor in my Achillies inflatable boat, I was reminded of the day we left Puerto Plata, on the Dominican Republic, heading for the Bahamas. The customs and immigration officers of the country were very concerned about their people stowing away on foreign ships to make the trip to the United States. Before we could sail, an inspection was required by the local officials.

At the time our dinghy was a 9-foot Zodiac Cadet which I bought used before our trip started. It hung on stern davits out in the tropical weather for several months. It was getting tired and leaked severely. Before going ashore I would pump it up and then take the pump with me to inflate it again when we headed out.

We were anchored in Puerto Plata about 100 yards off the dock and, after getting our clearance to sail, a very heavy local police officer, wearing heavy military boots, dressed in tropical whites and carrying a loaded AK47 over his shoulder, insisted on being taken to the boat to check it out.

I took a few minutes to pump up the boat as hard as I could and with trepidation invited the officer on board for the trip to the boat. I rowed as hard as I could with this nervous man in the stern shifting the AK47 from one shoulder to the other. What would he do to me if the leaking boat deposited him into the bay?

By the time we reached *Sunlit* the Zodiac had a noticeable sag and even stepping on the side was dangerous.

With a sigh of relief I made the boarding ladder and my passenger was able to climb aboard. While the officer made his inspection below, I quickly pumped up the inflatable again and made ready for the trip back. With great relief I was able to make it back to the government dock without getting him wet. I wonder how long I would have spent in jail if my little Zodiac had collapsed under us. Or even worse, does an AK47 fire underwater?.

6

AVALON

The two days in Little Harbor were very rewarding. With no other boats to disturb me I had plenty of time to outline more stories for the book. But time was moving on. I already was one day longer than planned for the trip. The store could get along without me for a while but I really should be there on the weekend when we have the most business. It was now Thursday and I was one day behind. Maybe it's asking too much to circumnavigate Catalina in a week and spend time in many of its little bays.

So after rigging the square topsail for easy hoisting, removing the gaskets from the mainsail and warming up the engine, I dropped down into the dinghy and retrieved the stern anchor. Hastily I got back to the boat before it could swing towards the rocks and began raising the main anchor. The electric power winch was a little difficult to use because the chain kept slipping off the gypsy. However, by keeping tension on the chain with my foot I was able to bring it in and break it loose from the bottom.

Because of the narrow confines of Little Harbor I did not take the time to raise the anchor and stow it on the bow pulpit. I let it dangle and motored out into deep water where I could leave the wheel in safety, haul the anchor up. and then stow it properly. The only problem with leaving the anchor hang was that it picked up a lot of kelp and it took quite a bit of time cutting it away. Anchors can be a nuisance but they are necessary.

Thinking about anchors opens up a whole world of tales to tell.

* * * * * * * * * *

HELMSMAN OR FOREDECK

He and his wife came into my store with an interesting request. "I need to find some kind of tool so my wife can handle the anchor chain easier." His wife was a very pretty lady who weighed about 120 pounds. He stood six foot three and was a very athletic-looking man. Then to top it off the skipper explained that his wife had lost two fingers on her left hand when she got her hand caught in the anchor chain of their 40-foot Bayliner powerboat. She quietly held up her mutilated hand.

The hackles rose on the back of my head. This customer had hit a very sensitive nerve. I have preached for years to my customers about the big burly skippers sitting behind the wheel or up on the flying bridge of their big yachts while the little woman runs around with the boat hook and ropes, fending off or trying to pull a 20-ton boat into the dock.

The skipper handles throttle and gearshift levers that require about 3 ounces of pressure to operate while the mate pulls in the 60 pound anchor or tries to make a 3/8 inch chain stay on a windlass gypsy and if she loses her fingers, we have to find her a better tool to control the winch.

Well I'll give you a simple tool. Put the skipper on the foredeck and teach the mate to operate the gear shift and wheel. Let the male beast do some hard labor for a change.

* * * * * * * * * *

Now that that's off my chest, I'll get down from the preaching pulpit and head for Avalon.

One thing I can say is that my cruising has met the criteria that I have set forth. During the 2 years spent on the cruise of *Sunlit*, I only remember one time when I handled the boat when we approached a dock or got ready to anchor.

That one time was at Puerto Azul in Venezuela, and I managed to tear off the starboard side rub strake against the fuel dock with my skillful maneuvering of the yacht. After that my wife, Joan, insisted on taking the wheel while I fended off and handled the lines.

I was also the one that pulled the 45 CQR anchor and horsed it into its saddle on the bow pulpit. No one can expect a 125 lb. woman to do that job. I practice what I preach. Besides Joan never let me forget the 200 dollars it cost to replace the rub strake.

* * * * * * * * * *

Cruising with a family is not always love and happiness. Joan and I often were at odds on how and where to anchor or tie up. I liked to enter a bay and cruise around a little to find a good anchorage. Not Joan, she pulled into a bay, assessed the situation instantly and ordered the anchor down. This sometimes caused me to be a little irritated and I would not always jump to instantly.

84

Generally things would resolve themselves once we were safely anchored and had a chance to relax. However the time we entered Golfito Bay in Costa Rica, things kind of bubbled to a head. I think it started earlier in the day when I suggested we try to sail the boat around a point without the engine. My racing instincts were strong and I wanted to test the boat on a beat in about 25 knots of wind. This time we would be macho sailors not stinkpotters.

This turned out to be a bad idea. *Sunlit* was not a racing boat and I could not make enough headway to windward to round the point. After several passes and many dark words from Joan, backed up by the kids, I reluctantly turned on the engine, rolled up the jib and motored towards our next port of call, Golfito.

I was unhappy. Why the hell couldn't I sail this boat. All it would take was some encouragement from the crew, but no they wanted to get into port. Sailing was not their thing.

I was still stewing a bit when we rounded up into the bay and began looking for an anchorage. Joan took over the wheel and ordered me up on the foredeck to drop the anchor. She headed up near some other boats and yelled for me to lower it. I wasn't sure it was the best place so I signaled her to go around again. She was forced to swing the boat around but also gave me a good tongue lashing at the same time.

She headed toward the same spot and yelled, "drop the god dammed anchor." I dumped the whole thing over the side and without another glance went below and mixed a drink. This wasn't very intelligent, and that evening we paid the price.

After a good dinner we had both relaxed enough to forget the earlier frustrations and had invited a couple from a boat anchored near by to come over for some cards. They made some remark about our little show when we came in and we all had a good laugh about it.

We were having a good time and didn't pay much attention to the rain and rising wind outside. That is until I looked out the port hole and saw a boat quickly going past us. I wondered why it was moving about in this weather and went on deck to check things out.

It wasn't the other boat that was moving, we were. The wind was very strong and visibility in the rain was nil. We were dragging our anchor and drifting backwards at about five knots. We had already left the anchorage and were well out into the bay.

While Joan started up the engine, our guest and I rushed to the fordeck to hoist the anchor. It was extremely heavy and when we horsed it aboard we found out why. It was one great big ball of anchor, chain and rope. No wonder it wouldn't hold. It was all tangled up. When I had dumped it overboard earlier, it all fell into one big pile, and we had not stretched it out and set it properly. It took us over twenty minutes to motor back to the anchorage, lay out the anchor and set it securely. In the heavy rain and wind we were soaked to the bone.

That night over eight inches of rain fell, several houses, on the cliffs overlooking the bay, tumbled down the hill and two people in the town were killed by landslides. The lesson is obvious one can't afford to be caught up in personal pride when you,re out cruising in strange waters.

* * * * * * * * * *

There was another time that I had trouble getting the anchor to hold. It was also frustrating but not nearly as dangerous. It was in the Berry Islands just east of the Great Bahama Bank of the Bahama island chain. We sailed into Frazers Cay and pulled as close as we could to shore. It was nice clear water, about 8 feet deep.

I laid the anchor down and let out 60 feet of chain and line. A good seven to one scope. Then we backed down to set the hook. It wouldn't hold. We just motored backwards, dragging it with us. I pulled it up close letting it hang straight down. We again moved up close to shore and tried again. Still it would not hold. We repeated this process about four times. Finally I jumped overboard with a snorkel, determined to set the anchor by hand.

Diving down I discovered the point of the CQR firmly imbedded into a conch shell. A live one at that. I removed the conch and set the anchor. Returning to the boat we cleaned the conch for dinner. I must say a 45 lb. CQR makes a hell of a fish hook.

* * * * * * * * * *

With the anchor safely stowed, *Iwalani* motored along the shore of the island. The wind was calm and the smooth sea was undulating with the large Pacific swells that pounded on the rocky shore. The white foam and spray is spectacular along this rugged shore.

The high cliffs of the Palisades loomed on the port side of the boat. In a strong westerly this is a weather bound-coast but when the Santanas blow, (the winter northeasters that scream off the mainland and make the other side of Catalina a very dangerous lee shore), this is the best protection and usually calm.

It was this area that was used by the seventeenth and eighteenth century sailors for protection from the northeasters that blew just as hard in that century. Henry Dana describes in his book, *Two Years Before the Mast*, being blown out of San Pedro Bay and taking shelter behind Catalina Island. In those days there were no safe harbors between San Diego and Monterey. It is also said that pirates lay in wait off Catalina for the Spanish galleons from Japan and China, as they crossed the Pacific Ocean bound for Panama.

* * * * * * * * * *

These thoughts of pirates brought back the memories of two occasions where I might have run across some pirates. I really am not sure. Let me tell you the tales.

PIRATES?

My family and I, aboard *Sunlit*, were on the passage from Huatalco, Mexico to Corinto, Nicaragua. We were about 50 miles off the entrance to the Gulf of Fonseca. It was the midnight to three watch and Joan was in the cockpit while I tried to take a snooze down below in the main cabin. Scattered rain squalls lit by the occasional lightning bolt passed over us as we headed south under sail without running the engine. Between squalls we drifted without much headway.

We had seen the lights of an occasional ship on the horizon but none were close. Joan's scream of "Bill get up here!" brought me up in an instant. "There a boat out there, close by with no lights," she told me and as we starred into the darkness a bolt of lightning lit up a gray motor cruiser, showing no running lights, about two hundred yards off our port quarter, heading on our course, apparently stalking us.

I went down into the cabin and turned on all our exterior lights and also took a flashlight to shine at the boat. I wanted him to know we saw him and to be sure he saw us. Then turning on the engine I headed the boat toward a nearby rain squall.

The mysterious boat followed us for another thirty minutes and then turned on its running lights and veered off into the darkness. We watched as his stern light disappeared behind the rain.

The next day we entered Corinto, Nicaragua and tied up to the government dock to present our papers and enter the country. The dockmaster directed us to tie up along side a patrol boat much like the unlighted boat from last night. I asked the officer of the day if it was one of these boats that scarred us so badly last night. He assured me it was not their boat but it could be any one of the three countries that border the Gulf of Fonseca. I asked him about piracy and he said, " Let me assure you there was no danger, there are a few shrimp fisherman who might steal each others shrimp but they wouldn't harm you." I wasn't very assured.

I can't blame these people for patrolling their waters, I just wish they weren't so sneaky.

There was another scare for the crew of *Sunlit*. It was on the crossing from the San Blas Island to Cartahena, Columbia. It was a hundred and fifty mile run from Plyon Chico to the Columbian coast.

We had left the village in the afternoon to be well clear of the San Blas Islands by dark. That night had been uneventful and we were sailing on a close reach under power and sail with about 25 knots of wind. This weather held into the next day.

About mid morning we spotted two motley looking motor vessels on an opposite course from ours. We had seen many of the Columbian boats in the San Blas Islands. They buy coconuts in the Islands and transport them to Cartagena. Some of these boats are terribly beat up and have a very unseamanlike appearance.

The first boat passed us close aboard and we waved at the six or eight rough looking man as we went by. They waved back in a friendly manner. All was fine until the second boat made a hundred and eighty degree turn in front of us and took up a course in the same direction as ours. I looked back at the boat that had just passed and they had come about behind us and were following our course. We were bracketed.

This I did not like. Why would two boats heading for the San Blas turn around and place us between them? We weren't that friendly. I decided this could be dangerous. We were one hundred miles at sea in waters that are often said to be dangerous with a history for hundreds of years of piracy and high seas terrorism. Was I a fool to put my family in such danger? Maybe I was. How do we get out of this?

The first thing I did was to crank the engine up to full speed and head off to a beam reach. We were doing over 9 knots in the rough choppy waters, sailing on our fastest possible course. I then went into the cabin and loaded the flare gun. This scarred my kids but it was the only firearm we carried. Next I took the microphone of my ham radio and tried to make a visible show of using the radio, hoping the crew of the threatening boats would see it. At the time I could not raise any one on the radio but I hoped the Columbian boats would not realize that.

The next few minutes were very tense until I realized that we were out running the two boats. At the speed we were moving, we soon overtook the boat that had turned in front of us and we were leaving the other boat in our wake. In the choppy seas we were faster than they were. In five more minutes we had shown that they could not catch us. With what appeared to be a friendly wave the first boat bore away and both boats resumed their course westward.

Were they pirates? Did they mean us harm? We will never know, however, later in Cartahena I saw a large cruising sailboat with bullet holes in the side and stripped of much of its gear. I understand it had run into a drug smuggling operation off the coast of Columbia and was attacked.

* * * * * * * * * * *

Motoring around the east end I came up on the famous town of Avalon. I eased into the busy harbor and was met by a harbor patrol boat who led me to a mooring a few rows from the outside and about five cans in from the main pier. It took a few minutes to secure the schooner fore and aft and I was soon relaxing in the cockpit with a cup of coffee.

I put on my best going-to-town clothes and flagged down the shore boat for the 100 yard ride to the pier. As I walked up to the main sidewalk I met an old friend. Carl was a marine salesman for the main supplier of Dad's Marine. We are great friends and have worked together for years.

Carl is a powerboat man and often jumps in his boat just to come to Avalon for lunch. This trip he was over making sales calls on the marine stores of the island. Seeing him reminded me of the trip we made on his little 24 foot ocean speed boat from San Pedro to Avalon.

A SHORT FLIGHT TO AVALON

He had invited three of his good customers to run over to Catalina for breakfast. We met at his boat, docked in San Pedro, and were soon out in San Pedro bay. "Hang on, everybody," Carl yelled over the roar of the engine, and thrust the throttle forward. The boat leaped ahead and we tore out the Angel's Gate, past the San Pedro light house, at about 50 miles per hour. My knuckles turned white and my breath was short but, boy! were we moving over the calm seas.

We were about halfway across the Catalina Channel when a large set of waves appeared on the bow. The boat was crossing a ship's wake. Flying off the first wave, we missed the second one and slammed into the third. Carl had seen the waves coming and tried to throttle down but we still hit doing about 40 knots. The boat was designed for the stress with its V bottom and ocean going hull, but I had been siting on the motor box and when we hit I smashed through the 1/2 inch plywood cover. I wasn't hurt but I was a little shook up.

Seeing that no one was killed, Carl rammed the throttle ahead and we were in Avalon only 30 minutes after leaving San Pedro. What a change from my five hour trip in *Iwalani*.

Taking up a mooring next to the pier, we ferried the 10 yards to the dock paying the $1.50 each to go 30 feet. We agreed that on the way out only one person would go to the boat and the rest of us would be picked up at the dock.

93

We walked up the pier and found our breakfast house right at the base. Over pancakes, sausage and eggs we discussed the flight over. After about 45 minutes we went back to the boat and roared away. Thirty minutes later and ten more white knuckles we were back in San Pedro, tied up at the dock and ready to go to work on another business day. The only problem was that my knees were still weak. Now you might understand why I am afraid of fast boats.

* * * * * * * * * *

Carl and I made plans to meet later in the afternoon for dinner. Then he went off to make his sales calls. I wandered along the beach front and soon was caught up in a shopping spree in the little stores facing the beach. I found a very nice shirt printed with the chart of Catalina and decorated with line drawings of Tall Sailing Ships.

At five o'clock I met Carl at the bottom of the steps leading to a fine Mexican restaurant high up on the hill, overlooking Avalon Bay. The food was superb and the view of my small tall ship riding in the bay made me long to head out and sail to Tahiti. I'll never do it but the dream is there.

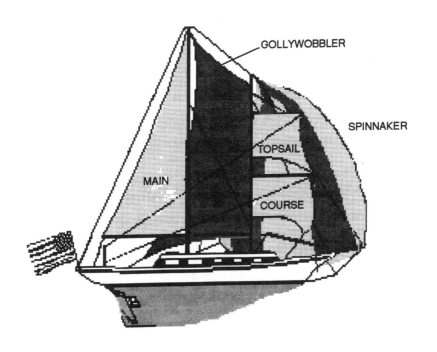

IWALANI

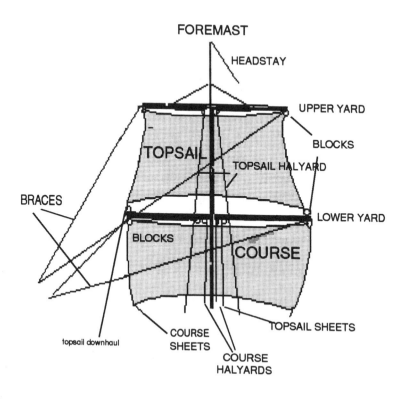

FOREMAST

HEADSTAY

UPPER YARD

BLOCKS

TOPSAIL

TOPSAIL HALYARD

BRACES

LOWER YARD

BLOCKS

COURSE

TOPSAIL SHEETS

topsail downhaul

COURSE
SHEETS

COURSE
HALYARDS

7

THE SAIL HOME

This has been quite a week. Six different anchorages in seven days. Catalina circumnavigated, a great party at Cat Harbor and a quiet couple of days in Little Harbor. After that a great dinner in Avalon, no serious problems for the week and a great many memories.

And now its time to head home. So up-an-at-it by eight o'clock. I have a quick breakfast and clean up the interior for the ride home. The weather looks just right for the trip. The sun is out with no clouds or fog, a rarity in May. The light southwest winds in the harbor foretell a westerly for the afternoon, probably not very strong.. How often do you get perfect weather for the passage you plan to make?

On deck I worked to rig the sails for easy handling. I hanked the big blue gollywobbler to the mast track. The squaresail halyards and sheets were rigged to the spars and the sails folded on deck ready to hoist. I decided to leave the genoa in its bag and instead hooked the spinnaker up on the bow pulpit. I fly this cruising chute with no pole, securing the windward corner to the bow pulpit and rigging a sheet aft to the cockpit. Anticipating the wind on a port tack, I rigged the sheet for the starboard side. Then after shackling the halyard to the head of the sail, I secured the spinnaker bag on the pulpit. It was ready to hoist but still out of the way.

Single-handing a boat like this takes some preparation. It is necessary to plan ahead and do things slowly. You can get into trouble if things get out of hand and you run out of time and space. Don't sail a boat rigged like this in close quarters.

But I have the whole Pacific Ocean, at least a good chunk of it between Catalina and Newport. It looks like a friendly wind and I have all day to sail the 32 miles from Avalon to the jetty entrance.

The Perkins started with the first touch of the button and while I let it warm up at idle for a few minutes, I prepared a light lunch for later. I figured I would not be able to spend much time down below while sailing and I had no deckhand to fetch and carry. OK, the boat is ready to go.

On deck I slipped the stern line off the cleat and, going forward, let go the forward mooring line and watched it drop into the depths. It is not a good idea to wind it into the prop. Quickly I made my way back to the wheel and after the boat had drifted backward a few feet, away from the mooring, I eased the gear into forward. With a wave to my neighbor on the next mooring, *Iwalani* slipped down the row and reached the main channel, I felt light and relaxed as we passed the breakwater entrance and pointed northeast towards home.

The wind was already swinging to the west but still very light. Locking the wheel on course I moved to the mainmast and soon had the mainsail hoisted and swinging lightly on a loose sheet. I set the forestaysail and returned to the cockpit to trim the sheets for a beam reach. I expected the wind to go even further aft soon. The Perkins still hummed along and we were doing about four knots in the calm seas.

By ten we were about a mile off the island and had cleared the lee of Long Point. A light swell rolled by from the west and the wind filled in at about five or six knots, enough to ripple the water but no little white caps.

Time to sail. I cut the engine and moved up to the foremast. The square topsail was easy to hoist. The upper corners are shackled to the halyards which are rove through blocks at each end of the yard, lead to the mast and then down to the deck. It is easy to grab hold of both at once and haul away.

After they are raised one side is cleated down and tension is applied to the other corner and the sail sets flat along the yard, secured at both upper corners and loose in the middle.

The sheets are rigged to the lower yard in the same fashion and, after a slight adjustment, are cleated down. The sail is trimmed to the wind by use of afterguys attached to the ends of the yard.

The lower square sail, or course, is rigged in the same manner except the sheets are cleated down to the deck. The afterguys adjust for the wind and the boat will sail with the wind aft to a few points forward of the beam. This is a down-wind rig that is simple to adjust once the sails are up.

We were now sailing as a brigantine schooner. This is certainly not a racing rig and not very efficient by today's standards, but it gave me great satisfaction to lay back and gaze up into square-rigged sails.

I admired this rig for a half hour or so even though we were not really tearing up the ocean in speed. I estimated we were doing two or three knots. Time to put on more sail. I had the gollywobbler already hanked on the foremast track with the fore halyard rigged. All that was necessary was to fasten the main halyard, hoist the foremast halyard first, trim the main halyard like a sheet and then trim the lower sheet. In the light air this is easy. Be careful when the wind picks up. Now my little ship had a very non- traditional look with square sails and a modern gollywobbler light air sail. Why not make it even more bizarre and fly the spinnaker.

All it took to get the spinnaker flying was to undo the top of the sail bag, hoist the halyard and sheet it home. Now we had some sail area up. For a while I just sat back and enjoyed the power of the boat under me. By this time the wind was just abaft the beam. It took a few minutes to trim the various sheets and afterguys to balance the boat to the optimum. *Iwalani* had no weather helm and it was very light on the touch. In the six to eight knot winds we were doing about four knots. Time to kick back and enjoy.

My thoughts went back over the past week. How often does it happen that things work out as well as they did this week. I was able to bring to mind many tales of my sailing experiences. I was able to organize this book. I planned my sail and sailed my plan. This was very satisfactory. I even think I found a place for my little poem *FOLLOWING SEAS* I'll insert it after this chapter. It describes today almost to a tee.

* * * * * * * * * *

It was close to four o'clock when I sighted the stacks of the Huntington Beach power plant and soon after I made out the Newport Beach jetty entrance. With about two miles to go I decided it was time to lower the sails.

When you single-hand, do things well ahead of time. The wind was about 12 knots and I could have my hands full if I was not careful. When sailing off the wind, the wind strength can fool you. The wind can build up quite a bit while you are lulled by the easy down-wind sailing. When it comes to changing course things can get real hectic as the boat heads closer to the wind.

The first sail down was the spinnaker. I let go the clew fastened to the bow pulpit. It flew like a flag out in front of the boat. With no wind filling the chute, it was an easy job to gather it in and stuff it in its bag.

The problem with the gollywobbler was to dodge the flaying halyards as I pulled it down from the mast. Getting hit with a metal shackle in the head is no fun.

However it was soon down and safely secured to the cabin top. I took a few minutes at the wheel to bring the boat back on course and then moved forward to lower the square sails.

First the lower course was taken in by releasing the two upper halyards and pulling the sail in with the sheets. The topsail was a little different problem. To pull it down I had rigged a line as a downhaul and when the sheets and halyards were released this downhaul allowed me to horse it down to the deck where I rolled it up and stuffed it below. In five minutes I was down to the main and foresail and in complete control.

By this time we had less then a mile to the jetty entrance. I decided to set the main staysail, and under these three lowers, I sailed the rest of the way to the jetty at a slow but steady pace. I again sat back and relaxed. We soon passed through the jetty entrance into calm water.

As we turned the corner to head up the bay the wind went forward. I tightened the sheets and, because the three lower sails were all on self-tending booms, it was no trouble to tack up the bay by merely turning the wheel. Not as fast as the sleek racing sloops that were also beating up the bay but we made good headway. It took about 30 minutes to make it to the edge of the mooring field where I keep the boat. Time to crank up the engine, drop the three sails and pick up my mooring. It was the end of a perfect week.

FOLLOWING SEAS

ILLUSTRATED
BY
ROB McNAUGHTON

FOLLOWING SEAS

RUNNING ALONG IN FOLLOWING SEAS
RUSHING DOWNWIND IN A VIOLENT BREEZE
THESE ARE THE THINGS THAT MAKE ME SO PLEASED
TO BE AT SEA AGAIN

CAREFULLY STEERING OFF THE CURLING WAVE
SLIDING DOWN INTO A CAVERNOUS CAVE
IT'S DAYS LIKE TODAY THAT MAKE ME CRAVE
TO BE FREE AGAIN

THE BOW MUST BE BUOYANT TO RISE FROM THE FOAM
FOR WITH THE WIND AT OUR BACK WE KNOW WE CAN ROAM
THOUGH THE WAVES MAY BE HIGH THEY COME FROM OUR HOME
AND WE"RE OUTWARD BOUND AGAIN

THERE IS A DIFFERENCE YOU SEE WHEN YOU'RE SAILING FREE
FOR WITH THE WIND AT YOUR BACK YOU DON'T HAVE TO TACK
AND THOUGH THE WAVES MAY BE HIGH THEY HAVE A BENEVOLENT CRY
AND YOU'RE OUT WHERE YOU WANT TO BE AGAIN

THE BOAT IS A PUSSYCAT AS IT SAILS ALONG
THE WAVE MAKE A HISS AND THE WIND SINGS A SONG
THE BOW SPRAYS LIKE WHISKERS SPREAD TO THE SIDE
AND I SHOUT IT OUT LOUD "WHAT A HELL OF A RIDE"

I KNOW IF I TURN TOWARDS THE WIND SHE'S A TIGER
AND I REALLY DON'T WANT TO BE RIDING ASTRIDE HER
FOR DOWNWIND IS NICE AND THE SEAS ARE MORE FRIENDLY
TO BEAT HARD TO WEATHER IS NOT WHAT EXCITES ME

THE RIGGING IS TAUT AND THE SAILS DO NOT SHAKE
AND WE'RE MOVING ALONG AT A DIZZYING RATE
I'LL SING YOU A CHANTY, I'LL YELL YOU A TUNE
FOR WHEREVER WE'RE GOING WE'RE GETTING THERE SOON

SQUARE UP THE YARDS AND EASE OFF THE SHEETS
IT'S NOT VERY OFTEN YOU ARE ALLOWED SUCH A TREAT
TO RUN WITH THE WIND IN FOLLOWING SEAS
AND TO BE OFFERED SUCH A GIFT AGAIN

BILL McNAUGHTON

EPILOGUE

Well, I have sold Her, *IWALANI*, my small tall ship. She is a Cheoy Lee, Clipper 42, schooner rig, to which I have added two yards, making her a Brigantine Schooner. She presently resides in Gig Harbor, Washington with her new owner.

Dad's Marine, the retail store is closed. Sadly my good friend Carl Beruto has passed away and he will be missed.

I have retired to a small house on a hill overlooking the Hood Canal and the majestic Olympic Mountains of western Washington State. It has given me time to reflect on my experiences of 40 years playing with boats.

However, I'm not done yet. The other day I spotted a beautiful little 27 foot Maine Lobster boat. It has a speed of about 12 knots, using a 80 hp diesel. I am working on a cabin layout for sleeping one or two. It just might be great for a few trips up the Alaskan Marine Highway and inland waters of Puget Sound. I'll let you know what happens.

One hour out of Avalon

THE AUTHOR
"I Alwaysliked this picture,
but the kids said I looked like a bum"

ACME PACK
DISTRIBUTING COMPANY
38035 Buck Road N.E.
Hansville, WA 98340
(360) 638-1278

c/o BILL McNAUGHTON

Specialized Marine Products
Marine Books

ORDER FORM
FOR
BOOKS AVAILABLE FROM
ACME PACK DISTRIBUTING
AND PUBLISHING CO.

# ORDERED	LIST PRICE	TOTAL
_____ TALES FROM A SMALL TALL SHIP BILL McNAUGHTON, AUTHOR	$11.95	_____
_____ SAILING ILLUSTRATED PAT ROYCE, AUTHOR	$12.00	_____
_____ SAIL COURSE PAT ROYCE, AUTHOR	$12.00	_____
_____ POWERBOAT ILLUSTRATED PAT ROYCE, AUTHOR	$15.00	_____
_____ BOAT COSMETICS MADE SIMPLE SHERRI BOARD, AUTHOR_	$12.95	_____
_____ THE RACING GALLEY COOK BOOK GOLDIE, JOSEPH, AUTHOR	$14.95	_____
_____ THE COASTAL COMPANION JOE UPTON, AUTHOR	$16.95	_____
_____ THE BURGEE DAVID KUTZ, AUTHOR	$22.95	_____
_____ SAILING THE GOLDEN SEA PAUL KELLER, AUTHOR	$14.50	_____
_____ SAILING THE INLAND SEAS PAUL KELLER, AUTHOR	$14.95	_____
Washington State residents add 8% sales tax.		_____

SEND ORDERS TO: TOTAL   _____
ACME PACK DIST. & PUBLISHING CO.
38035 BUCK RD.N.E.
HANSVILLE, WA 98340
(360) 538-1278

ACME PACK
DISTRIBUTING COMPANY
38035 Buck Road N.E.
Hansville, WA 98340
(360)
638-1278

CALL BILL McNAUGHTON

Specialized Marine Products
Marine Books

ORDER FORM
FOR
BOOKS AVAILABLE FROM
ACME PACK DISTRIBUTING
AND PUBLISHING CO.

# ORDERED	LIST PRICE	TOTAL
_____ TALES FROM A SMALL TALL SHIP BILL McNAUGHTON, AUTHOR	$11.95	_____
_____ SAILING ILLUSTRATED PAT ROYCE, AUTHOR	$12.00	_____
_____ SAIL COURSE PAT ROYCE, AUTHOR	$12.00	_____
_____ POWERBOAT ILLUSTRATED PAT ROYCE, AUTHOR	$15.00	_____
_____ BOAT COSMETICS MADE SIMPLE SHERRI BOARD, AUTHOR_	$12.95	_____
_____ THE RACING GALLEY COOK BOOK GOLDIE, JOSEPH, AUTHOR	$14.95	_____
_____ THE COASTAL COMPANION JOE UPTON, AUTHOR	$16.95	_____
_____ THE BURGEE DAVID KUTZ, AUTHOR	$22.95	_____
_____ SAILING THE GOLDEN SEA PAUL KELLER, AUTHOR	$14.50	_____
_____ SAILING THE INLAND SEAS PAUL KELLER, AUTHOR	$14.95	_____

Washington State residents add 8% sales tax.   _____

SEND ORDERS TO: TOTAL   _____
ACME PACK DIST. & PUBLISHING CO.
38035 BUCK RD.N.E.
HANSVILLE, WA 98340
(360) 538-1278